A WOMAN'S GUIDE TO

SPIRITUAL POWER

THROUGH SCRIPTURAL PRAYER

NANCY L. DORNER

A WOMAN'S GUIDE TO

SPIRITUAL POWER

THROUGH SCRIPTURAL PRAYER

NANCY L. DORNER

STARBURST PUBLISHERS

P.O. Box 4123, Lancaster, Pennsylvania 17604

To schedule Author appearances write:
Author Appearances, Starburst Promotions, P.O. Box 4123,
Lancaster, PA 17604 or call (717) 293-0939

Credits:
Cover Art by Bill Dussinger
Unless otherwise noted, or paraphrased by the author, all Scripture
quotations are from the King James Version.

First Printing, September 1992

ISBN 0-914984-47-0
Library of Congress Catalog Number 92-60587

Printed in the United States of America

Dedication

This book is dedicated to the men in my life–
they have made this book possible:

For *Ken,*
my patient, wonderful husband who has supported
me and my dreams for nearly forty years;

For *Jeff,*
without whose diligent efforts this book would
never have been published. Jeff has always been
one of the greatest blessings of my life;

For *David,*
whose encouragement and faith has helped
me over all the rough spots;

For *Brian,*
whose gentle prodding kept me climbing
whenever I was tempted to give up;

And for *Jesus Christ,*
the Incarnate Word, my Lord, Savior, King, and
Friend, without whom none of this would be!

In the beginning was the Word, and the Word
was with God, and the Word was God . . . . And
the Word became flesh, and dwelt among us . . . .
John 1:1 & 14

Thanks be to God!

Table of Contents

Summary of Chapters

Note: Thirteen chapters, including the Introduction, are suitable for an adult Sunday School quarter. Each Chapter is followed by a "For Reflection" Section, Study Questions, and a list of applicable Scripture References.

INTRODUCTION

Does God Answer Prayer?; (A cynical atheist discovers through a series of Prayer "Experiments" that God is real, God cares, and God answers prayer.)

CHAPTER ONE

Why Pray?; (If God loves us so much, why should we have to pray? Which prayers does God honor, and why? What admonitions does Scripture make in reference to prayer?)

CHAPTER TWO

Prayer & Christ-Centeredness; (Putting God first in everything; Living the Christ-centered life.)

CHAPTER THREE

Prayer and Sin; (Confession of sin and repentance is necessary for a vital, satisfying, and productive prayer life.)

Index of Events and Topics

Foreword

Someone has wisely said, "There are no unanswered prayers; some are answered, 'Yes,' some 'No,' and the rest, 'Not yet.'" While many of my own prayers are answered, "No," or "Not yet," in this book I speak of those answered, "Yes."

Introduction

Why read a book about prayer?

Since prayer should be the cornerstone of our relationship to the Lord, it is important that we desire to strengthen that relationship.

This book has grown out of my over twenty years experience of answered prayers. A converted atheist, I was a new Christian when I first began my series of prayer "experiments." A dear friend and "spiritual mother" assured me that God is real; God cares, and *God answers prayer.*

The Lost Kitten

My first dramatic experience of answered prayer concerned a lost kitten. Our five year old son Jeff had been given a darling calico kitten with a curly tail. We named the kitten "Kinky." She was unusual looking and affectionate. Jeff loved her very much. He bought a pretty red leather collar with fake "jewels" on it for Kinky to wear. Once when we went on vacation the little girl next door took care of Kinky. When we returned, we learned that the little girl had let Kinky outdoors and she had run away.

Jeff was broken-hearted. But I reassured him, "Don't worry, honey; we'll find Kinky. She can't have gone very far. We'll search the neighborhood and knock on every door until we find her. I'll put an ad in the paper and one on the radio. Someone surely has found Kinky and is taking good care of her."

We went from door to door, leaving our telephone number in case anyone should find our lost kitten. No one had even seen her. And our ads in the newspaper and on the radio brought no results.

The following Saturday morning, when we were eating breakfast, we heard our ad on the local radio station. Jeff began to cry.

"Mommy, we'll never find Kinky. She's gone forever."

"Oh honey, I'm so sorry. I've done everything I know to do, except *pray* and . . . ."

I stopped short. I had forgotten to *pray* about the lost kitten. That should have been the *first* thing I did, but I was a new Christian, and not yet used to letting God help me with life's problems. So Jeff and I bowed our heads and prayed that God would return Kinky to us.

We had no sooner opened our eyes and raised our heads, when the telephone rang. It was a lady who lived across town.

"I just heard your ad on the radio," she said. "I've found a kitten. It doesn't match your description, but I thought if you hadn't found yours yet, your little boy might like to have this one. I can't keep it and I haven't been able to find its owner or anyone else who is willing to take it. Would you like to come and see it? Maybe it would help your little boy if he had another kitten."

I explained the situation to Jeff. Would he like to go and at least take a look at this kitten? He decided he would look at it–but he really wanted only Kinky. So we got in the car and drove to the lady's home on the other side of town.

We discovered that the kitten she had found looked nothing like our Kinky. It was a gray tiger of a very ordinary type. Jeff was not taken with it at all. So we thanked the lady, got back in the car, and started for home. We had gone just a few blocks when Jeff again began to cry.

"Mommy, maybe I *should* take that gray kitten. It would be better than no kitten at all. I don't think we're ever going to find Kinky."

So I pulled off to the side of the road and gave him a hug. Jeff said, "Let's pray once more, Mommy, and if God doesn't bring Kinky back right away, we'll go get the little gray kitten."

Once more we bowed our heads and Jeff, in his little boy quaking voice, asked God to send his kitten back RIGHT AWAY so he would not have to take the gray one.

To our amazement, when we opened our eyes, Kinky was sitting on the pavement not ten feet away from our car. Jeff jumped out of the car and ran to Kinky. I was almost in shock–we were still a long way from home.

God only knows how that kitten came to be there. I certainly don't. Without a doubt, it was our kitten; it had the same curly tail, the little red patent leather jewel encrusted collar, and the exact markings of our kitten. I was so stunned and so shaken that I could hardly drive home.

All the way home, I pondered this amazing answer to prayer and the sequence of events that had brought it about. Had we not gone to see the gray kitten on the other side of town, we would never have been driving down that particular street at that particular time.

Had God used that telephone call to put us where we needed to be, so we would find Kinky? Had God picked up the kitten from wherever it was, and set it down in front of us? Or was it just a coincidence?

I decided then and there, to make prayer my *first resource* rather than my *last* resort, and see if any other "coincidences" occurred as a result. With renewed enthusiasm, I intensifed my study of the Scriptures.

Originally, I had had a tendency to view the Bible as a mysterious collection of esoteric wisdom–something requiring great insight and persistence to understand all the "symbolism" contained therein. Then, a mature Christian friend suggested I try to accept it at face value, taking each command and promise as being a simple, easy to understand message instructing me how to live the Christian life.

My friend did not deny that there may be very profound symbolism in the Scriptures–however, she pointed out that I did not have to *understand* the principles it contained–I needed only to *OBEY* them. **No amount of esoteric insight will unlock the spiritual power of God's Word. Even the smallest attempt to BELIEVE and OBEY God brings immediate results in our lives.** She emphasized that Christianity is an *affair of the heart*–not a "head trip."

One of the biggest stumbling blocks to my spiritual growth was my pride; I thought I had to *understand* God and His Word before I could surrender my will to Him. Yet, although I *really* didn't know exactly what it was or how it worked, I used electricity and other mysterious sources of energy or power. Even the most common energy conversion, the utilization of food by the body, is an enigma to me.

How does an apple come to be? Exactly what transpires to combine minerals from the soil, sunlight and chlorophyll into the apple I eat? I can describe this process, but do I really understand it? When I eat the apple, how does my body break the apple down into its components and direct them to the necessary cells? How do the cells then process these materials in a way which is beneficial to the entire body?

People often tell me they do not believe in miracles-yet each person depends on "miracles" to sustain them in their everyday life. Miracles abound. They are all around us.

Some of the miracles which I have experienced in response to prayer, are just a continuation of the miraculous life process we experience daily. *One is no more incredible than the other.*

The more I studied the Bible, the more my respect for its contents continued to grow. Yet, there were passages which utterly perplexed me. Jesus said, *Ask anything in my name, and I will do it.* (John 14:12, 13)

Yet people suffer and die-in spite of sincere prayers and devout living. Why? If God is who He claims to be; if the Scriptures are accurate records of His instructions, what is wrong? These questions disturbed me.

I decided to read every piece of literature I could find on prayer, hoping to find someone who could explain it to me. In my attempt to understand, I prayed for insight and wisdom, then continued to "pore" over the Scriptures. But the process remained as obscure and mysterious as ever.

Eventually, I would begin to have some ideas which might be considered insights. For the present, however, I continued to pray, watch and wait for answers. Not *all* of my prayers were answered immediately; *not all* were answered, "Yes." But many were. Many prayers were answered immediately and positively. (These answers will be recounted as we study together what I found in the Bible.)

LIFE can become an amazing adventure as we learn to walk with the Lord and daily exercise the privilege of prayer.

Chapter One

Why Pray?

Be careful (anxious) for nothing; but in every thing by prayer and supplication with thanksgiving let your requests be made known unto God.

Philippians 4:6

Pray without ceasing.

I Thessalonians 5:17

If God loves us so much, and wants only the best for us, why should we have to pray? If He loves us, why does He allow suffering to come into our lives? We all have asked these questions at one time or another.

Why does God command us to pray? Why does He not answer "Yes," right away? I believe one reason is that God is far more interested in our *ultimate holiness* than in our *immediate happiness*.

Looking back on my own life and the prayers answered, "No," or "Not yet," I can see quite clearly what the Lord has done. But at that time, I simply could not understand His withholding from me the desires of my heart. After all, His Word declares, *Delight thyself in the Lord and He will give you the desires of your heart.* (Psalms 37:4 NIV)

Why then does He not grant our every wish? Probably for the same reason we don't grant every wish of our children. We are far more interested in their growth and development than in their immediate gratification.

The Bible warns us that at times God will seem like an unkind father, but He is not. I have to admit, at times God seemed that way to me—but hindsight has caused me to praise His wisdom and His loving kindness. How much more could I have pleased God had I, at that time, been able to praise Him.

It has taken me nearly two decades to attain any degree of maturity–and I am still not fully mature. But I would like to share with you what I have learned. Perhaps my sharing will help you grow faster than I did; I hope so. Others have helped me–perhaps I can repay their generosity by sharing with you.

We often expect to get ready answers to our prayers *before* we have put God's instructions into practice in our lives. Oftentimes, because He is so gracious, God answers the prayers of new or young Christians *before* they have thoroughly read and applied His "instruction manual," the Bible. At times it seems that God leaves our prayers hanging in the air, perhaps desiring us to be moved to deepen our understanding of Him and His ways.

I remember how as a new Christian I felt completely overwhelmed at my own ignorance in relation to the immensity of the Scriptures. To read the entire Bible, and understand what it all meant for my life, seemed an almost impossible task. Fortunately, I met two women who were knowledgeable in the Scriptures and, because of their faith and obedience, had a vibrant and vital personal relationship to the Lord.

It was they who led me through the Bible, pointing out that what I needed was to develop a meaningful relationship to Jesus Christ. They assured me, that once I seriously began to study and *apply* the Scriptures, I, too, would begin to get astonishing answers to my prayers.

Growing In Prayer

1. Pray for an ever-deepening relationship with Jesus Christ, asking God to help you surrender your entire life to Him.

2. *Daily* pray for an anointing by the Holy Spirit, and for wisdom and insight as you study the Scriptures.

3. Pray for discipline and self-control as God reveals His will for your life, as you struggle (it will be a

struggle sometimes), to make what you *do* measure up to what you *know*.

Why do we pray? We pray because we have a natural longing to commune with the lover of our souls. The Bible stresses the importance of prayer. Jesus told us to pray. St. Paul admonishes us to pray *always*.

Someone has wisely said, "If you don't feel as close to God as you used to, guess who moved?"

God has promised to reward our efforts to establish a closer relationship to Him. James 4:8 tells us, *Draw nigh to God, and he will draw nigh to you* . . . .

We establish a close relationship to God exactly as we establish one with anyone else–by spending time with them. The more *quality* time we spend with the Lord, the closer we will feel to Him. When we love someone, it is a delight to be in their presence; we *want* to be with them.

I had no desire to get to know God until I was 35 years old. I was an outspoken atheist. (I did not believe God existed.) My husband, the son of a Lutheran pastor, was an agnostic. I believe my husband's disillusionment with the church was based on the hypocrisy, backbiting, and powerlessness he had observed while growing up.

When I was 32, an *agnostic* challenged me by saying there were *two* kinds of atheists: the respectable, informed type, who had seriously searched for God; and the non-respectable, uninformed variety, who had never really searched the evidence, but had decided off the top of his/her head, that God does not exist. He scornfully declared that I was the latter type.

His scorn moved me to try to become a *respectable* atheist. I began a search that was to take over five years, and included the Scriptures of all the world's living religions. But I found no convincing evidence for God's existence until I began to study the Bible, especially the New Testament.

Eventually, Jesus Christ was to bring me to my knees–thanks to what I read in the Bible and the additional witness and testimony of an eighty-two year old pastor's widow. As a dedicated atheist, I was perplexed by the promises and statements I found in the Bible. I had gone to a Christian pastor for clarification; too busy to answer all my questions, he led me to the Christian widow, whose amazing prayer life was to change my own thinking finally and dramatically.

Carrie was a diminutive, white-haired lady whose example was to convince me there are two kinds of Christians, as well as two kinds of atheists: those who enjoy a personal relationship with God in Jesus Christ; and those who just "belong to the church" but do not really *know* the Savior.

Carrie prayed about almost *everything*. Considered a *prayer warrior* by her congregation, she was often called upon to intercede for others. She kept a small spiral notebook in which she entered all prayer requests, noting the date the request was made.

When the prayer was answered, she noted that date in red, next to the original request. Carrie's prayer notebook was full of red letter days.

Amazed by the results she recorded, I expressed my skepticism. She responded by challenging me. "Isn't there something you need that I could pray for?" she inquired. "Surely there is something God could do to prove to you His authenticity and accessability? God loves even atheists and longs to make Himself known to them. But sin separates even the best of us from God.

"Our only approach to Him must be made through His Son, Jesus. Since you don't know Jesus, He will not respond to *your* requests. I know Him, love Him, and *obey* Him, to the best of my ability. The Lord and I are on good terms.

"Let me intercede for you. What would you like me to pray for? I'm already praying that God will reveal Himself to you."

There was one thing I longed for. My husband and I had been married for nearly fourteen years, and were (according to medical specialists), unable to have children. We had adopted a wonderful little boy named Jeff, and longed for more children. But at that time it was difficult to adopt a second child, and we were getting close to the cutoff age of eligibility. As a result, our hopes seemed doomed to disappointment. But according to Carrie, nothing was too hard for God.

"God knows many things the doctors don't know," she said, and continued to pray that we would have a child of our own.

On May 12th (Mother's Day) of 1968 our first biological son was born; we named him David (our beloved Jeff was then six years of age). Since we had moved back to our home state of Michigan, Carrie was no longer as available to instruct me.

Nevertheless, encouraged by this seemingly amazing answer to prayer, I continued to study the Scriptures and to try to understand them. Until I met Carrie, I had been a cynical, pessimistic atheist. I did not believe in answered prayer–because I didn't believe in God. But after following her directions (taken from the Bible), I was to become a firm believer and an avid practitioner of prayer.

I wondered (as perhaps you have), since God knows all our needs, why we should take the time to pray? Often, new Christians develop a similar attitude, and as a result, neglect to pray. Yet the Scriptures are clear. God commands us to pray.

Throughout history, the saints who have left a record of their spiritual lives have reaffirmed the importance of a vigorous prayer life. Over and over again, the records show that spiritual life is dependent upon two things: *prayer* and *obedience* to the Scriptures. One without the other weakens us spiritually; each feeds our souls.

Relatively few Christians develop a robust prayer life-thus not all Christians get the answers to their prayers which the Scriptures promise. Instead, they experience a spiritual *leakage* which often leads to a relatively *Spirit-less* existence.

The words of the hymn *What a Friend We Have in Jesus* express the ultimate fate of those who either cease praying, or who pray only occasionally:

> Oh what peace we often forfeit,
> Oh what needless pain we bear,
> All because we do not carry,
> Everything to God in prayer.

When our prayer life is weak, all of life is weakened-yet many of us have never known anything else and do not recognize our impoverished condition. We struggle through life with minimum joy, and experience countless struggles which an effective prayer life could banish-or at least diminish.

In His Word, God has given us everything we need to know about His *communication* system. Unfortunately, few of us have made an indepth study of what the Bible teaches on this all important topic.

The Scriptures have many *conditional* promises regarding answered prayer, promises contingent upon our *obedience*. Often when we read John 15:7, *If ye abide in me, and my words abide in you, ye shall ask what ye will, and it shall be done unto you.*

We fail to obey the *first* part of the verse and then wonder why the *second* does not take place. Yet, should we take these instructions seriously and *put them into practice*, our lives would spring into amazing adventures, full of inspiring *coincidences* and gratifying fulfillment.

For Reflection

Why Pray?

"No prayer means no power. Little prayer means little power. And much prayer means much power. Our world is in desperate need of that which only our Lord can do, and prayer is the force that moves the hand of God."

John Bisagno
The Secret of Positive Prayer, Pg. 8

". . . prayer is not easy. It is not the speaking of many words, or the hypnotic spell of the recited formula; it is the raising of the heart and mind to God in constantly renewed acts of love. We must go forward to grapple with prayer, as Jacob wrestled with the angel. We must lift high our lamp of Faith that it may show us what prayer is, and what are its power and dignity. Into the darkness we must whisper our prayer: Lord, teach us how to pray . . . it is a concept which will take us our whole life to fathom, and a practice which our whole life will be too short to perfect."

Karl Rahner
On Prayer

Questions for Discussion

Chapter One

1. If God knows all of our needs anyway, why should we pray about them?

2. At what point in your affairs do *you* begin to pray:
   A. Before beginning a new endeavor?
   B. When beginning a new endeavor?
   C. Halfway through a new endeavor?
   D. When and *if* things begin to go wrong?
   E. After everything has fallen apart?

3. What can you assume when God answers "No," or "Not yet," to your request?

4. Do you think God answers "foxhole" prayers? Why or why not?

5. Share some examples of answered prayers.

6. List three prayer requests you will be working with for the remainder of this study. Get a small spiral notebook in which to record your prayer requests and the date they are made. See what happens!

References

Why Pray?

Jeremiah 29:11-13
Matthew 6:5-13
Matthew 26:36
Matthew 26:41
Mark 6:46
Mark 14:32, 38
Luke 6:27-36
Luke 9:28
Luke 22:40-42, 46
Luke 18:1
I Timothy 2:8-11
I Thessalonians 5:17-18
James 5:13-15

Notes

Chapter Two

Prayer and Christ-Centeredness

Putting God First in Everything; Living the Christ-Centered Life

Delight thyself also in the Lord; and he shall give thee the desires of thine heart.
Psalms 37:4

Thou shalt love the Lord thy God with all thy heart, and all thy soul and all thy mind.
Matthew 22:37, Mark 12:30, Luke 10:27

How much do you love God?

On one occasion, after speaking at Christian Women's Club, I was approached by a woman who wished to talk with me.

"Mrs. Dorner," she said, "I just loved your talk. I'm a Christian, too. I've been one all my life, but I never get answers to my prayers like you have. Why not?"

"How much do you love the Lord?" I asked her.

"With all my heart." she replied. "I'd do *anything* for God!"

"Well, do you get up early and pray?" I asked. "I find the best time to talk to God is very early in the morning. Try getting up at 5:00 a.m. and spending at least one hour in prayer."

"Oh, I could *never* do that!" was her shocked reply. "I don't get up until about ten o'clock. I like to stay up and watch the late, late show."

Did she love the late, late show more than she loved God? I wondered. I'm not saying that one *must* get up early in order to get ready answers to prayer, but I *am* saying that we must have our priorities in proper order.

God has to come *first* in our life. He must be more important than ourselves, our families, our other interests. Yet we must give God our fullest devotion, without doing any *damage* to our other relationships.

One way to do that is to get up very early (before anyone else) and spend time with God. By the time the rest of the family is up, you are ready to give to them all the love God gave to you in your early devotional time with Him. **One hour of prayer is worth two hours of sleep.**

Let us ask ourselves, "Do we love God as much as we love sleep?" Until we love Him enough to structure our day around Him, our prayers will likely be only half-hearted attempts to influence God, rather than *wholehearted attempts to commune with God and to know His will for our life.*

Many times our prayers seem to be attempts to get God to perform like our celestial *errand boy. God is not an errand boy!* Such prayers get about as much attention as they deserve. However, when we order our lives according to God's plan we *then* will become God's errand runner.

Several years ago, God burdened me with concern for one of my son's music teachers. My son asked me to go see this young man on **His** behalf. Since I didn't know the young man very well, and since I don't usually try to minister to men, I asked my husband to take our son and me to hear the teacher perform at a certain restaurant.

During a "break," the teacher came over to our table to chat. We noticed that something was obviously wrong; the young man was visibly depressed. When we expressed our concern, he said only that he was having "family problems." When the "break" was over, we had little time to talk with him.

On our way home I urged my husband to write the teacher a note expressing our concern, offering to help him in any way we could. This my husband did. Later, I tried to reach him by telephone to invite him to dinner. This way we would have an opportunity to talk. There was no answer at his home, and after several tries, I called the store where he conducted his lessons and left a message for him. That weekend we left for a vacation.

A week later, when we had returned from our vacation, I read in the newspaper that this talented, personable young man had committed suicide. We learned that three times that week he had called a crisis center for help; each time he got a different person; no one gave him the help he sought. Upon talking to several of his associates, we learned that his wife had left him, taking their young children with her. The teacher had obviously felt alone and unloved. Had I been able to give him the message that God loved him, the man might still be alive today.

This incident impressed upon me the importance of following God's leading; of being willing to be His *errand girl* when called upon to do so. I remembered that, "we are God's hands and feet." It is not enough to just pray that he will bless the needy of the world–He expects to do it through us!

We must reach out to feed the hungry, clothe the naked, comfort the sick, visit the prisoner. Many times God working through us brings answers to prayer. If we are not willing to be a *blessing to others,* we have no right to expect God to bless us. When we get into a right relationship with Jesus Christ we will find His blessings abounding in our life.

How much do *we* love God? Enough to put ourselves at His disposal? Enough to make time for Him and His Word? *Daily devotional time is essential!* Not that we can't pray while in the shower, driving to work, or anywhere else. We should; but if we are to be of any use to God time reserved for Him alone is vital.

We cannot have a personal relationship with anyone unless we are willing to give of ourself and our time. *God is no exception.* Anyone who would know Jesus must *spend time alone with Him!* He must become the most important person in our life.

The Bible promises, *Draw nigh unto God and He will draw nigh unto you* . . . . (James 4:8)

In an adult Sunday School class I once heard someone remark that it was foolish to pray for little things like a parking place.

"God doesn't want to know about such trivia," was the comment.

I don't think it matters whether He *wants* to know– He *does* know. If God is everywhere (omnipresent and all pervasive) He is with us constantly, and therefore knows everything that is happening to us.

If it is true, as the Bible says, that . . . *in Him we live, and move, and have our being* . . . . (Acts 17:28) and if our bodies are the "temple of the Holy Spirit," then we truly cannot get away from God. He will never leave us nor forsake us. (Hebrews 13:5B) So, if we're looking for a parking place, God knows all about it.

When my youngest son, Brian, was about seven years old, he was invited to a friend's birthday party. I had forgotten to get a gift for him to take, so we left early Saturday afternoon, intending to stop at the mall and select a gift. But the mall parking lot was full. We drove around and around looking for a place to park.

Finally Brian said, "Mommy, let's pray for a parking place. If we don't get one soon, I'll be late for the party!"

So we bowed our heads and asked God to make a space for us. When we opened our eyes, the car immediately on our left pulled out, and I pulled into the newly vacated space.

"Wow," said Brian, wide-eyed, "God sure gives quick service, doesn't he?" "Well, no," I thought, "Not always. But He does give *good* service."

Is it terribly self-centered to expect God to be concerned about such a trivial thing? It seems to me the critical thing here is our attitude and our relationship to God. If we're doing as Jesus told us to and are "praying always," we will automatically hold *everything* up to God.

Paul also urged us to *pray without ceasing.* Over and over he assured the Christian community that they should pray about everything. (Philippians 4:6, Ephesians 6:18, I Thessalonians 5:17)

John also stressed the importance of prayer: *And this is the confidence that we have in him, that, if we ask anything according to his will, he heareth us: And if we know that He hear us, whatsoever we ask, we know that we have the petitions that we desired of him.* (I John 5:14-15)

If, however, a Christian prays *only* when in a pinch or when he wants a *favor* from God, he is not obeying Scripture, and is in danger of becoming very self-centered – the exact opposite of what Christ is calling us to do. *If anyone would be my disciple let him **deny himself**, take up his cross daily and follow me.* (Matthew 16:24, Mark 8:34, Luke 9:23) Anyone who prays *only* at the "parking place" level is making prayer a pretty petty practice. But the Christian who carries on a running dialogue with the Lord is as apt to pray for a parking place as for peace–yet each topic will automatically get the time and attention it deserves.

If our priorities are in order, this matter takes care of itself. Certainly, it is better to pray about too much than too little–and I fear we are more in danger of doing the latter than the former.

When should we pray? Any time, all the time. Jesus himself implied this. In one instance, He instructed his disciples that when they prayed they should go into their closet and shut the door, and pray to their father in secret. But He also said, *For where two or three are gathered in my name, there am I in the midst of them.* (Matthew18:20)

Surely we *need* to spend time alone with God. But we *also* need to participate in communal prayer. I cannot think of any situation where prayer is inappropriate or out of place.

Where should we pray? In our "closets" certainly, but also anywhere we feel the need or desire to pray.

There are many times during the day, while carrying out routine duties, when we can easily carry on a conversation with God at the same time, much as we carry on conversation with family or friends while so engaged. But that should *not* be the extent of our praying.

Again, at least one hour alone with God every day–early in the day–is the best time for most of us. God should come *first* on our schedule. God should come second on our schedule. And God should come last on our schedule! We need to close our day as we started it–on our knees, in the presence of God.

If God isn't *everything* to us, He is in danger of becoming *nothing* to us. In this area Moslems have an advantage. The entire Moslem community is *called* to prayer five times a day!

Where should we pray? Everywhere.
When should we pray? All the time.
What should we pray about? Everything.

By being in constant communion with our Lord, through prayer, we show that we love Him as we are commanded to do: *You shall love the Lord your God with all your heart, mind, and soul.*

For Reflection

Prayer and Christ-Centeredness

"Religious persons and students of religion agree in testifying that prayer is the center of religion, the soul of all piety."

Friedrich Heiler
The Essence of Prayer, Pg. 316

"Those who would learn this fine art of prayer must desire it more than anything else in life. They must firmly believe that by finding the true meaning of prayer all other meanings will be enhanced. Faith so directed and acted upon brings forth fruit."

Edgar N. Jackson
Understanding Prayer

"The purpose (of prayer) is not just to get out of difficulties or solve problems or deal with troublesome people. All that will happen, but the greater result will be that we will come to know and love our God more profoundly as a friend.

Lloyd Ogilvie
Praying with Power

"Where shall the world be found, where will the Word resound? Not here, there is not enough silence."

T. S. Elliot
Ash Wednesday

"Christians aren't perfect–just forgiven."

Bumper Sticker

Questions for Discussion

Chapter Two

1. If we tithed our *time* as well as our other assets, how long would we spend in devotions each day?

2. Is "devotional" time *all* God asks of us? What about ministering to the hurting and needy in our community? In our neighborhood? In our family?

3. Where might you "invest" your time and energy in Christ's name?
    A. Church (Teaching, nursery, choir, kitchen duties, groundskeeping, newsletter, communion preparation, library duty, floral and altar arrangements, bulletin collation, office help, other?)
    B. Gospel Mission participation
    C. Youth Ministry/Jail Ministry
    E. Habitat for Humanity
    F. Soup Kitchen/*World* Hunger programs (Bread for the World, etc.)
    H. World Vision (Child Sponsorship)
    I. Missions: Support of Missionaries and/or volunteering your services.

4. How can you express your love for God while working on various other tasks? (i.e., by singing hymns, listening to tapes, memorizing Scripture, etc.)

5. What are you willing and able to give up in order to spend more time in prayer, praise, study, and other devotional practices? (i.e., watching TV, reading newspapers, magazines, or books not related to spiritual growth, bowling or other sports, "idle" conversation, hobbies, etc.)

6. Is your love for God evident to all who know you? (If you were arrested by the enemy for practicing Christianity would there be enough evidence to convict you?)

References

Prayer and Christ-Centeredness

John 15 (note verse 7)
John 6:51-69
John 14:6, 12-14, 21
John 16:13-14
Matthew 7:21-27
Acts 4:12
Romans 8:38-39
Colossians 3:17
Ephesians 5:20
Ephesians 2:18
Galations 3:26
James 1:22

Notes

Chapter Three

Prayer and Sin

Confession of Sin and Repentance are Necessary for a Vital, Satisfying, and Productive Prayer Life.

If I regard iniquity in my heart, the Lord will not hear me.

Psalms 66:18

If we confess our sins, He is faithful and just to forgive us our sins, and to cleanse us from all unrighteousness.

I John 1:9

Prayer is communion with God. It is not "using" God or getting Him to do *our will*. Only when we make a serious attempt to do *God's will* are the channels of communication open between us.

Prayer has become my number one priority. This is due to many years of prayer. I wish I could understand and explain it, but it is a mystery now as it was when I first began exploring it. However, I have learned something as a result of all my study: *God is utterly reliable!*

When things go wrong, most often it is *we* who have failed–not God. Sometimes it seems God is far away or completely non-existent. But when this seems to be the problem, I have learned to search *myself* to see why. As I've said before, "If God doesn't seem as close as He used to, guess who moved?"

Unfortunately, contemporary society has all but forgotten God, and sin is a concept which is almost totally ignored. Yet if sin is ignored, God becomes inaccessible to us. God does not want to *ignore us,* but He *cannot ignore sin.*

When sin is rampant, as it is today, it erects a shield between us and God. We *cannot* penetrate this shield, and God *will not* penetrate it, except through the blood of Jesus Christ. If we ignore God's provision for sin, we then have no access to Him or His blessings. We sin, and then overlook our sin, at our own peril!

It is unconfessed and unrepentant sin that separates us from God. But, praise be to God! If we are in Christ, and spend time in daily confession, it need separate us no longer.

Many of us present only our "persona" (our ego or false self) to God, confessing some insignificant or even significant lapses as the sum of our sin, ignoring sins that we have "hidden away," then wondering why there is no change in our circumstances. God is not nearly as interested in changing *our circumstances* as He is in *changing us*!

Becoming whole (holy) requires complete surrender to Christ. Until we confess our hidden sins, we cannot walk in true fellowship with the Lord. *For all have sinned, and come short of the glory of God.* (Romans 3:23)

As the psalmist, we must cry out to God, *Examine me, O Lord, and see if there is any wicked way in me.* (Psalms 139:24 Paraphrased)

Draw nigh to God, and he will draw nigh to you . . . .(James 4:8)

We must *strive* to live holy lives but recognize that we will fail. And when we *do* fail we must turn to God in repentance to receive His forgiveness. The Bible promises, *the effectual fervent prayer of a **righteous** man availeth much.* (James 5:16) To have confidence that our prayers will be answered, we must seek righteousness. While we know that we often fail, we continue in our prayers.

In Exodus we read about God supplying manna to the Jews in the wilderness. Every day a fresh supply of manna was provided. But the people could gather only *one day's* supply at a time. If they gathered too little they went hungry; if they gathered too much, it spoiled by the next morning. It had to be gathered on a *daily* basis.

We are to journey through life in this manner-one day at a time. God never gives us a month's, or even a week's supply of grace in advance. That is why a daily, disciplined prayer time is so essential-and confessing our sins must be a part of that prayer.

The Bible also states, *If I regard iniquity in my heart, the Lord will not hear me.* (Psalm 66:18) If we desire God to hear and answer our prayers, we *must* repent of the iniquity (sin) within us.

Another requirement for answered prayer is a forgiving attitude. In the prayer given to us by Jesus we are instructed to say *and forgive us our debts (sins), as we forgive our debtors (those who sin against us.)* In other words, God will not forgive us if we are holding a grudge against someone else.

We must view others with compassion if we expect God to view us that way. In Chapter Eight we will take a closer look at how important our relationships to others are in an effective prayer life.

For Reflection

Prayer and Sin

"To confess your sins to God is not to tell Him anything he doesn't already know. Until you confess them, however, they are the abyss between you. When you confess them, they become the bridge."

Frederick Beuchner
Wishful Thinking, Pg. 15

"Self-confrontation (is) absolutely essential: we cannot, must not, hide from ourselves; we must face the worst of ourselves (or our shadow) and acknowledge it. The higher morality requires confronting the shadowy one within us who has made the rules necessary in the first place."

John Sanford
The Kingdom Within, Pg. 51

"As long as men are inwardly in conflict, divided within themselves, victims of their own inner opposition, they are easy prey to evil. But where the kingdom of God is being established in an individual, he is also becoming whole and the kingdom of evil has no power over him."

John Sanford
The Kingdom Within, Pg. 57

"It is those who have recognized that they have been injured or hurt in some way in life who are most apt to come into the kingdom. Unless a person has recognized his own need, even his own despair, he is not ready for the kingdom, as those who feel that they are self-sufficient, who life has upheld in their one-sided orientation, remain caught in their egocentricity."

John Sanford
The Kingdom Within, Pg. 68-69

Questions for Discussion

Chapter Three

1. Do you think the world takes sin more casually now than it did fifty years ago? Why or why not?

2. Do you personally take sin less seriously now than before you became a believer? Why or why not?

3. Is there any danger in taking sin too casually? Is there danger in taking it too seriously?

4. The Bible admonishes us to "confess our sins to one another." Have you ever "confessed" to another person? What is the value of such confession? What are some safeguards we should employ when we confess to another person?

5. Is confessing to God *all* we really need to do to clear our guilt? Why?

References

Prayer and Sin

Psalms 32:3-6
Psalms 37:4-11
Psalms 66:16-20 (note verse 18)
Psalms 139:23-24
Ezra 9:5-6
Isaiah 1:10-20
Isaiah 59:1-2
Jeremiah 7:8-23
Ezekiel 18:19-28
Daniel 9:3-14
Matthew 6:19-34
Matthew 23:13-14
Romans 3:10-23
Romans 6
Romans 14:16-23
Mark 12:38-44
Ephesians 4:17-32
Ephesians 5:1-18
James 4:1-17
James 5:15-18
I John 1:8-10
I John 2

I John 3:17-24
Psalms 51

Notes

Chapter Four

Prayer and Faith

Why is Our Faith Necessary for God's Answers? What is faith?
How do We Get it?

. . . According to your faith be it done unto you.

Matthew 9:29

Now faith is the substnce of things hoped for, the evidence of things not seen.

Hebrews 11:1

And call upon me in the day of trouble: I will deliver thee, and thou shalt glorify me.

Psalms 50:15

But without faith it is impossible to please Him: for he that cometh to God must believe that He is, and that He is a rewarder of them that diligently seek Him.

Hebrews 11:6

61

In the New Testament Jesus proclaims over and over again to those He has healed, *your faith has made you whole.* Yet many of these suffering ones had been ill or crippled for years before their encounter with Jesus (i.e., the man at the pool of Bethsaida, the woman with the issue of blood.) Why had their faith not worked previous to meeting Jesus? Obviously there was something very *compelling* about Jesus that increased and elevated their faith to an effective level.

In one sense, it was much easier to be influenced by Jesus when He walked the earth–He could be seen, heard, and touched. In another sense, it was more difficult. Only those in his *immediate presence* could benefit from Jesus' power.

Now, via the activity of the Holy Spirit, anyone who calls out to Him or reads His *Word* (Bible) has access to this same power. But the Word must be read in *faith*, and acted upon in such a way that it becomes a part of one's day to day experience. This is neither an easy nor a short-term endeavor.

If Jesus put so much emphasis on faith, it must be indispensible–but how do we get faith? In Romans 10:17 we read *so then faith cometh by hearing, and hearing by the Word of God.* So we're back to the importance of the Scriptures.

In order to get answers to prayer, we must *believe* we will get answers, and to keep our faith at an effective level, we must spend time every day in . . . the Word. (James 1:6)

A group of which I was a member was about to embark on a new unit of Bible study. The book of Romans was suggested, whereupon one lady replied, "I read Romans once years ago. Can't we study something I haven't already read?"

Such an attitude toward the Bible will never lead to a dynamic Christian experience. No matter how many times we read the Bible, it always has more for us the next time. True, the book of Romans, for example, is the same each time we read it–but *we* are different. And each time we read it, we bring different perceptions, different strengths, different weaknesses, different needs. Therefore, each time we read it, our insights into its truth will be deepened. Continual Bible study is essential to a Christian's growth and faith.

As I said earlier, I became a Christian as a result of trying to become a "respectable" atheist. After my conversion, I learned that there are *two* kinds of Christians as well as *two* kinds of atheists.

As I became acquainted with more Christians, this distinction became evident. Some seemed vibrantly alive, aglow with love, peace, and joy–an inspiration to all with whom they came in contact. It could truly be said that *rivers of living water* flowed from them. They refreshed everyone they met.

But not all Christians were like this. As a matter of fact, most of them were not. Most seemed as weighed down by life's problems, and empty of joy, as the atheists and agnostics of my acquaintance. What is the reason for this?

After spending much time with each type of Christian, I discovered the reason: the majority of Christians knew *about* Jesus and even more *about* the church; but the more vital Christians *knew Jesus Christ PERSONALLY.*

Many languid Christians have been church members all their lives, but have never seriously entered into a personal relationship with the living God. They simply don't *know* Him and are in danger of being told at the final judgment, *Depart from me. I never knew you . . . .* (Matthew 7:21 NIV)

Those who *knew* the Savior seemed to get much more dramatic and affirmative answers to their prayers. They prayed much more frequently and with *greater wisdom* than did the others. They were much more spiritually mature. Their prayers were not attempts to manipulate God and get Him to do *their* will. They were sincere attempts to learn *God's* will for their life and to *live* it. One such radiant, obedient Christian was Carrie.

When I asked Carrie how one could *know* the Lord, she recommended I start by reading and *putting into practice* the fifteenth chapter of John. She suggested I especially note the number of times Jesus spoke of *obedience.* Only by taking these words of Jesus very, very seriously would I progress in the spiritual life. And only when I had made a sincere effort to grow spiritually would I develop an effective and meaningful prayer life.

Carrie pointed out that for most Christians prayer is only a last resort. Many of us are what Carrie referred to as "fox-hole pray-ers." Prayer is not so much something we *do*, as something we *are*.

Prayer is meant to be *at-one-ment* with God. And since Jesus had endured the cross to become our *atonement* (at-one-ment) we must now let Jesus live in us. How do we do this? By following the directives in John 15 and "abiding in Christ" and letting His words *dwell richly in us.* I challenge anyone to memorize John 15, reflect seriously on it for one half hour per day for thirty days, and not be changed dramatically by it.

We often hear people quote Jesus' promise, *ask whatever ye will in my name, and I will do it for you.* We rarely hear the first part of that verse, however: *If ye abide in me, and my words abide in you . . . .* (John 15:7) Until we satisfy the first condition, the second will not follow.

Try this experiment: read John 15 slowly and prayerfully, and spend at least *fifteen minutes* every day in meditative reflection on these words, asking the Lord to instruct you in His will for your life. OBEY His advice. Then see what happens.

Some people think faith comes from miracles, but others know miracles come from faith.

A small congregation in the foothills of the Great Smokies built a new sanctuary on a piece of land willed to them by a church member. Ten days before the new church was to open, the local building inspector informed the pastor that the parking lot was inadequate for the size of the building. Until the church doubled the size of the parking lot they would be unable to use the new sanctuary.

Unfortunately, the church with its undersized parking lot had used every inch of their land except for the mountain against which it had been built. In order to build more parking spaces, they would have to move the mountain out of the back yard.

Undaunted, the pastor announced the next Sunday morning that he would meet that evening with all members who had "mountain moving faith." They would hold a prayer session asking God to remove the mountain from the back yard and to somehow provide enough money to have it paved and painted before the scheduled opening dedication service the following week.

At the appointed time, two dozen of the congregation's 300 members assembled for prayer. They prayed for nearly three hours.

At ten o'clock the pastor said the final, "Amen." "We'll open next Sunday as scheduled," he assured everyone. "God has never let us down before, and I believe He will be faithful this time."

The next morning, as the pastor was working in his study, there came a loud knock at his door. When he called, "Come in," a rough looking construction foreman appeared, removing his hard hat as he entered.

"Excuse me, Reverend. I'm from Acme Construction Company, over in the next county. We're building a huge new shopping mall over there and we need some fill dirt. Would you be willing to sell us a chunk of that mountain behind the church? If we can have it right away, we'll pay you for the dirt we remove and pave all the exposed area free of charge. We can't do anything else until we get the dirt in and allow it to settle properly."

The next Sunday the little church was dedicated as originally planned–and there were far more members with "mountain moving faith" on opening Sunday than there had been the previous week.

Would you have shown up for that prayer meeting? Some people say faith comes from miracles. But others know: *miracles come from faith.*

For Reflection

Prayer and Faith

"A miracle is an event or action that apparently contradicts known laws of science."

Webster

"Worry is like a rocking chair; it gives you something to do, but it doesn't get you anywhere. Don't worry. Pray!"

Anonymous

". . . faith has substance and reality. It acts and does and accomplishes because it believes God and takes Him at His word. *Faith is being willing to stretch higher than you can reach.* Faith is being willing to risk, to dare, to dream. Faith is not believing God *can*, It is believing God *will*. And that, even now, it is as good as done."

John Bisagno
The Secret of Positive Praying, Pg. 15

"A scientist's view on such subjects as God, morality, life after death, are apt to be about as enlightening as a theologian's views of the structure of the atom or the cause and cure of the common cold. The conflict between science and religion, which reached its peak toward the end of the last century, is like the conflict between a podiatrist and a poet. One says that Susie Smith has fallen arches. The other says she walks in beauty like the night. In his own way each is speaking the truth. What is at issue is the kind of truth you're after."

Frederick Beuchner
Wishful Thinking, Pg. 86

"Shocked and startled that Freud considered telepathy to occur, Jones exclaimed, 'If we are prepared to consider the possibility of mental processes floating in the air, what is to stop us from believing in angels?' Freud replied, 'Quite so; and even de liebe Gott!'" (The living God)

Ernest Jones
The Life and Work of Sigmund Freud

Questions for Discussion

Chapter Four

1. What events and practices cause your faith to grow? What causes it to shrink? Do you think we are responsible for keeping our faith firm and steady? How can we do this?

2. Have you had any experience where your faith made a significant difference in decisions you have made or actions you have taken?

3. Were your parents or someone else important in instilling and nurturing your faith? Who was your "Carrie?" How did they influence you?

4. Has your faith influenced anyone else to believe? Your children? Neighbors? Colleagues? Others?

5. Have you regularly memorized Scripture verses so His words will "dwell richly" in you? Have such verses been helpful in times of stress or crisis? In times of gratitude and celebration? Do you encourage your children to memorize Scripture? How can this be done most effectively?

References

Prayer and Faith

Matthew 6:25-34
Matthew 8:5-13/23-27
Matthew 9:2, 22, 27-29
Matthew 13:54-58
Matthew 14:25-32
Matthew 15:28
Matthew 17:14-21
Matthew 21:18-22
Matthew 23:23-24
Mark 10:51-52
Mark 11:22-25
Luke 5:20
Luke 7:6-10, 50
Luke 8:24-25
Luke 17:5-19
John 14:12-14
Romans 4:15-25
Romans 8:28-32
Romans 14:22
Hebrews 11 (note verses 1-6)
James 1:19-27, 4:1-17, 5:15-18
I John 5:13-15

Notes

Chapter Five

Prayer and God's Guidance

Does God Have a Plan for Our Lives?
Can We Know His Will?
What is Divine Guidance?

For I know the plans I have for you, says the Lord. They are plans for good and not for evil, to give you a future and a hope.
                                    Jeremiah 29:11 (LB)

"Why doesn't God give us explicit directions so we know what He wants us to do? How can I possibly figure out His will for my life?"

A college student friend of mine was confused and undecided about a career choice he needed to make. He wanted to do the Lord's *will*, but was uncertain how to know *His* will. My friend came to me for help

73

with his problems, and although I couldn't assure him that God would send him a personal letter or a telegram to show him the way out of his dilemma, I could point out to the young man that God has written a personal "love letter" of instruction which is available to all who are willing to read it.

God's Word, the Bible, is His love letter and instruction manual to His children. As we study and apply His directives in the Word, *divine guidance* for all of life's decisions becomes available to us.

For I know the plans I have for you, says the Lord. They are plans for good and not for evil, plans to give you a future and a hope. (Jeremiah 29:11 LB)

If we obey His spiritual laws, God has promised to answer our requests for guidance. His *spiritual* laws are as immutable as His *physical* laws. We know that if we drop something, it will fall down, not up. Similarly, if we follow God's spiritual instructions, we *know* He will guide, comfort, and protect us. His Word promises this.

One day when Jeff was three years old, I put him down for a nap, and then began to clean my bedroom closet. I had taken everything out of the closet and was vacuuming the interior, when Jeff woke up and toddled into my bedroom. "Mommy, I'm hungry," he said. "Can I have something to eat?"

Exasperated that I hadn't finished my task before he awakened, I curtly told him, "Hold your horses, honey. I'll be finished in a few minutes; then I'll get you a snack."

He gave me a puzzled look before toddling back to his own room. In a few minutes he was back, clutching his toy pony, a small statue of a horse, and his book about horses in his arms. He had taken my admonition to "hold his horses" literally and seriously!

And that's exactly what God expects us to do with His Word. We must take Him literally and seriously if we want His guidance in our lives.

Our first step is to seek God's will–then do it. We must *know* and *do* that which He has *already* revealed to us before He will give further guidance. The Scriptures tell us, *Your words are a flashlight to light the path ahead of me, and keep me from stumbling.* (Psalms 119:105 LB) We need to use God's flash light constantly.

In addition to studying the Bible, we must seriously examine our life. Plato made the statement, "The life that remains unexamined is not worth living." We need to put ourselves right with God by eliminating sin from our lives.

Isaiah 30:21 tells us, *And thine ears shall hear a word behind thee, saying, This is the way, walk ye in it.* . . . God's still, small voice is heard only by the obedient and the sensitive.

Each of us has been individually designed by the Creator for a specific purpose. It is up to us to examine ourselves and try to discern this purpose. Not only our strengths and assets are a part of the divine design, but our weaknesses and faults also need to be assessed as well. Together, these form a kind of "in-born guidance system" we must heed.

When my husband was seeking guidance for his vocation he did an examination of his strengths and weaknesses. At the top of the list of weaknesses was the tendency to be overly perfectionistic. Thankfully, he then discovered a profession where this "weakness" would be a highly prized asset–he became a plastic surgeon.

Yes, when our "weaknesses" are carefully examined and turned over to God, they can be converted into strengths. What may seem a liability in our eyes, God may be able to use as an asset.

Several years ago, one of my students exasperated me by constantly doodling in class. He had a packet of felt tip pens in various colors and all during my lecture would draw elaborate designs. He was an apathetic student, and when I gently chastised him for his inattentiveness, he apologized, saying, "I'm never going to amount to anything. All I ever want to do is doodle."

When I took a closer look at his "doodles," I suggested he send these gorgeous arrangements of abstract design to a textile designer. He was hired as a designer and now happily spends his days "doodling." What he considered a waste of time, God turned into a real career.

Proverbs 3:6 tells us, *In all thy ways acknowledge him, and he shall direct thy paths.* One time, on a trip to New York City, I decided to take this verse very seriously. I drove from Atlanta, GA to Kennedy Airport without a map of any kind, trusting God to guide me. (I never was good at reading maps.)

I never got lost, and whenever I doubted my direction the Lord supplied someone to tell me exactly what I needed to know to reach my destination. He is faithful, and we are not disappointed when *we* are faithful to Him.

Part of being faithful includes confessing our sins. The Bible tells us, . . . *a broken and contrite heart, O God, thou wilt not despise,* (Psalms 51:17) and further assures us, *If we confess our sins, he is faithful and just to forgive us our sins, and to cleanse us from all unrighteousness.* (I John 1:9) Remember, when we confess our sins and repent, God honors our prayer requests.

God also guides us through Godly persons. When we face major decisions, we need to seek the counsel of a pastor, a Christian counselor, our families, or trusted, mature Christian friends who have a good knowledge and understanding of God's Word.

Malachi 2:7 (LB) reminds us, *Priests' lips should flow with the knowledge of God so the people will learn God's laws. The priests are the messengers of the Lord of Hosts, and men should come to them for guidance.* Our pastors and other mature Christians are our "priests," and we should seek and heed their advice.

In addition to studying God's Word, being faithful in confession and prayer, and heeding Christian counsel, we need to be sensitive to subtle leadings or directions from the Lord.

One summer I drove to a certain city to speak. The meeting was to be held at a motel there. I naively had assumed they would have a room for me, but the motel was completely full-as was every other motel in the city. After checking about half a dozen others, I finally bowed my head and quietly asked God what I should do. Surely *He* knew where I would find a vacancy.

Immediately following the prayer, I got the impression I should return to the first motel. When I walked up to the desk, the clerk was on the telephone-taking a cancellation. I got the room because I had heeded God's "guidance" and was first in line. Such leadings from the Lord are frequent, but we sometimes fail to heed them.

If we have earnestly sought God's will, we will then make decisions based on the wisest choice, as we discern it, and then give the Lord time to confirm or check the choice. James 1:5 tell us, *If any of you lack wisdom let him ask of God that giveth to all men liberally and upbraideth not; and it shall be given him.*

Recently I needed some information for an article I was writing, but had forgotten the last names of several students who could do research for me. I prayed that, within the week, God would make this information available to me. Three days later, I received a letter from one of those students, who remembered all the names I needed. Such answers to direct requests are common among God's people.

But in order to get such specific answers, we also must heed James 1:6: *But let him ask in faith, nothing wavering. For he that wavereth is like a wave of the sea driven with the wind and tossed.*

If you don't ask with faith, don't expect the Lord to give you any solid answers, for you can never please God without faith. (See Hebrews 11:6A.)

James 4:2 tells us, . . .*ye have not because ye ask not.* . . . This includes requests for guidance. Stay close to God always in all things, for the Bible clearly says, *Draw nigh to God, and He will draw nigh to you* . . . . (James 4:8) Only when we are close to God can we expect to receive His guidance.

Yes, He does guide and direct us–*even when we are unaware of His guidance.* As Dr. Robert Cook, former President of Kings College, put it: "He guides us in our steps, in our stops, and in our stumbles."

But He will not send you a telegram or write His message on your walls. He has already written you a long love letter–the Bible.

Remember, *In all thy ways acknowledge Him, and He shall direct thy paths.* (Proverbs 3:6)

The importance of attentiveness to God's guidance is illustrated by this story about the great Methodist Missionary, Dr. E. Stanley Jones:

Jones spent two weeks each year travelling from city to city in India to raise funds for his Mission. In an attempt to gain their financial support, he scheduled three talks each day to prominent citizens. He would address one group at breakfast, a second at lunch, and a third at dinner. The next day he would repeat his appeals to three groups in another city.

One night, after his third presentation, he rushed to the airport where he had booked the last flight of the day to his next day's destination. As he stood in line to get his seat assignment, they announced that his flight was oversold. They then requested that passengers give up their seats in return for an additional free round trip ticket to the city of their choice.

When the agent had finished his announcement, Jones thought he heard the Lord whisper to him, "Step out of the line." He hesitated. But he knew that if he didn't take this flight he would miss at least two meetings the next day as well as the money he hoped to raise. He stayed in line.

When he was near to the podium he again felt God urging him to step out of line and give up his seat. Again he hesitated, not sure if it were God speaking to him, or only his imagination. But when he was just one person away from the airline agent, he again heard God speak, this time in no uncertain terms: "STEP

OUT OF THE LINE!" Jones obeyed and someone else took his place.

The airliner crashed, killing all that were aboard!

When the media learned that Dr. Jones had not been aboard the airplane, they rushed to interview him. When told why he had not been aboard the ill-fated flight they were incensed.

"Do you mean to tell us that you were the only one God loved enough to warn?" they asked incredulously.

"Oh no!" came Jones' quick reply. "I don't mean that at all! I know God loved every person aboard that plane at LEAST as much as He loves me. But, you see, I was the only one who was listening."

Are we listening? Or have we forgotten how? Do we only know how to talk TO God? What we say to Him is important, but not nearly as important as what He wants to tell us. Remember the words of the song *In The Garden:*

> And He walks with me
> and He *talks* with me. . . .

Although I may begin my prayer by asking God to do something for me, somehow He always turns the tables by asking me to do something for Him. God is not our celestial errand boy. In fact, anyone who listens to God will become HIS errand runner. Could that be one of the reasons we spend so little time in prayer?

For Reflection

Prayer and God's Guidance

But seek ye first the Kingdom of God, and His righteousness; and all these things will be added unto you.

Matthew 6:33, See Luke 12:31

. . . and be at peace: thereby, good shall come unto thee.

Job 22:21

"Grant that we may never seek to bend the straight to the crooked-that is, thy will to ours-but that we may bend the crooked to the straight-that is, our will to thine."

St. Augustine

"Prayer is not overcoming God's reluctance, it is laying hold of His highest willingness."

Archbishop Wm. Trench

"Prayer is rather a living relation of man to God, a direct and inner contact, a refuge, a mutual intercourse, a conversation, spiritual commerce, an association, a fellowship, a communion, a converse, a one-ness, a union of an 'I' and a 'Thou.' "

Friedrich Heiler
The Essence of Prayer, Pg. 311

Questions for Discussion

Chapter Five

1. Do you agree that God "guides us in our steps, in our stops, and in our stumbles"? What does God do with our mistakes?

2. Have you ever experienced God's guidance but been unaware of it *at the time?* What finally made you realize that God had been guiding all along?

3. Do you see any danger in searching out God's will for your life? If yes, how can we insure against such danger?

4. Would you have done anything any differently if you had actively sought God's will before making some major decisions in your life? Do you think it is ever too late to turn your life over to God? Why or why not?

5. Have you ever experienced God's guidance so clearly there could be no doubt of His will in the matter?

6.   Have you ever *disregarded* God's clear guidance? What happened as a result? What was your response the *next* time you received such guidance?

References

Prayer and God's Guidance

Psalms 48:14
Psalms 51:17
Proverbs 6
Isaiah 58:11
Jeremiah 1:8
Jeremiah 29:11-13
James 4:8

Notes

Chapter Six

Prayer and Praise

Rejoice evermore. Pray without ceasing. In every thing give thanks: for this is the will of God in Christ Jesus concerning you.

I Thessalonians 5:16-18

Rejoice in the Lord alway: and again I say, Rejoice.

Philippians 4:4

My study of the Bible has taught me that God has created us for fellowship with himself. He wants us to know Him and enjoy Him forever. Psalm 37:4 reminds us that we are to take delight in the Lord, much as we delight in those we love. *Delight yourself in the Lord and He will give you the desires of your heart.* (NIV)

Just as we will do all in our power to satisfy a beloved (and loving) child, God will do all in *His* power to give us the desires of *our* hearts. How do we show someone we love that we delight in them? We praise them. We spend time and energy communicating our delight in them. Should we do less for God, the creator and sustainer of the universe? Surely, there is so much to praise God for that we should be able to expound endlessly on His marvelous nature.

When my son Jeff was about five, we went for a drive one Sunday evening. My husband and I were sitting in the front seat and Jeff was in the back looking out the rear window. Suddenly we heard him exclaim in a wonder-filled voice, "Oh, *thank you*, God!"

Looking in the rear-view mirror we discovered the source of his awe and praise–*a rose-gold sunset spread over the entire western horizon.*

I believe such spontaneous expressions of wonder and delight should be common in our day-to-day experiences. There is *much* to thank and praise God for, but we become blasé, and take such blessings for granted, forgetting to express our appreciation and gratitude to the Creator. We need to return to the attitude of wonder and awe of the little child, and to utter frequent expressions of these feelings.

One day while I was eating a banana, it occurred to me what a miracle a piece of fruit is–how does such a delectable morsel come from soil, sap, and sunlight? Thinking about the wonder of all such fruit I blurted out without thinking, "I'm so glad God went 'Bananas!' " This brought howls of glee from my children–but they got the message.

Everything that grows and produces "fruit after its own kind" is a source of wonder and delight. When we pause to think about it we cannot help but *delight* in the Lord. And God is as pleased with us when we respond this way as we are when our own children turn to us with expressions of gratitude and pleasure. Such an attitude is a prerequisite for a healthy prayer life.

When I started teaching at a state university, I was prepared to face the inevitable criticism I would encounter as a result of my belief. On the first day, as I stood placing my books in the tall bookcases provided, my office-mate, a man of my age, suddenly said, as I stood with my back to him, "I hear you're a Christian, Nancy. Now, tell me, you aren't one of those people who believe Jesus was some kind of god, are you?"

I had a few seconds to phrase my reply before I turned to him.

"No," I said, "I don't think Jesus was some kind of god."

"Oh, good!" he said with obvious relief, whereupon I rejoined with, "I think he is God incarnate."

"Oh, no! Not one of those." he moaned.

This was the first of many such discussions. We had our half-hour lunch break at the same time, and we each brought a sack lunch. Soon we began to share the lunch (We were both health food advocates) as we swapped opinions.

One day he asked me why we had placed our children in the Christian schools, when there were such excellent public schools in our area.

"What can the Christian school teach your child that the public school cannot?" was his question.

"An attitude of gratitude, wonder, and reverence," was my instant reply. He was silent as it registered that these were the very traits many children lack, and this lack is often the root of their poor attitudes, both at school and at home.

Our children, as a result of their Christian schooling, were usually appreciative and respectful. They did not take blessings for granted, were rarely rude to or disrespectful of parents, teachers, or even each other. Every day was started at home *and school* with prayers of gratitude and praise.

In their school, nothing was taken for granted, not sunrise nor sunset nor anything in between. God was honored as the creator of an amazing universe and our wonderful world. All day long, in history, science, math, social studies, sports, He was praised and thanked for His many blessings to us.

When children hear God praised at home, at church, *and* in school, their attitude usually becomes one of gratitude and reverence.

Such training pays off. We have had none of the widespread serious discipline problems in our Christian schools that plague public school systems across the country. Most of our young people go through adolescence fairly easily, knowing their rightful place in the family, the school, the world, and the cosmos. Their world view is rich with meaning, whereas many in the secular world do not even know their place in the family, much less in the cosmos.

This attitude of gratitude and reverence is essential to a meaningful life–and equally vital to a rich prayer life. When one meditates on the Word of God (both the written Scriptures and the incarnate Word, Jesus Christ) he cannot help but be overwhelmed with gratitude, wonder, and praise. It is impossible *not* to praise God–if we stop and think about Him.

And that's precisely what prayer is: *stopping to think about Him*. Taking time to be truly *present* with God, and His wonders, giving Him and His creation our undivided attention.

Since we are so busy, it would be easy to *forget* to praise God, to put off spending time alone with Him, *unless we deliberately discipline ourselves to do so regularly*. We may claim to love Him, in spite of being too busy for Him. But how many of us would believe our children *really* cared about us if they ceased to spend any time with us, or never bothered to say, "Thank you," or "I love you?"

In Philippians 4:6 we read Paul's admonition: *Be careful for nothing; but in every thing by prayer and supplication with thanksgiving let your requests be made known unto God.*

Sometimes it is easy enough to remember to pray when we need God's help–but not so easy to remember to thank Him. He probably feels much as we do if *our* children only come to us when they want something.

Therefore, we should form the habit of thanking Him daily for His blessings.

In I Thessalonians 5:18, Paul admonishes us *In every thing give thanks: for this is the will of God in Christ Jesus concerning you.*

Does this mean we are to thank God even for our tragedies and disappointments? Perhaps not-but we *are* to praise and thank Him *in* our tragedies and disappointments. For no matter *what* happens to us, life is a precious gift; and despite its problems, God deserves our adoration and gratitude *all the time!*

> This very minute has within it
> All I need of God and thou,
> The Really Real is really here
> And Eternity is NOW!

An exciting life of continuous adventure is available to all who appropriate the truth of the Bible. Don't just believe *in God,* BELIEVE GOD and become truly and completely alive. Enjoy the "abundant life" Jesus promises you!

But Seek ye first the Kingdom of God, and His righteousness, and all these things shall be added unto you. (Matt. 6:33) The man or woman who truly knows God in Jesus Christ never wants for anything-he may *lack* some things-but if so, he won't *want* them. There are two ways to be rich: have great wealth or few greeds!

Truly, God does give us the "desires of our hearts"–
that is, He puts the right desires within us. He then
satisfies all those desires for us. His name is Wonderful! Try Him! Find the truth for yourself and be truly
free.

I promise you, God will bless your efforts, for
"whoever seeketh, findeth." For every step you take
toward God, He will take three steps toward you.

For Reflection

Prayer and Praise

"More and more the spirit of 'nothing but' hovers over our advanced scientific research: the effort to degrade, disenchant, level down. Is it that the creative and the joyous embarrass the scientific mind to such an extent that it must try with might and main to degrade them?"

Theodore Rozak
The Making of a Counter Culture

"Worship in the ancient English means 'worth-ship,' or establishing the worth, the wonder, and the glory of God in our minds and hearts."

Lloyd Ogilvie
Praying With Power

"Nature as a whole is herself one huge result of the Supernatural: God created her. God pierces her wherever there is a human mind."

C.S. Lewis
Miracles

"All the books ever written do not have as many units of information on their pages as does the DNA (deoxyribose nucleic acid) molecule."

Henry M. Morris
That You May Believe

"All science nowadays sets out to talk man out of his present opinion of himself."

Frederick Nietzsche

"There is, I think, some truth in Nietzsche's remark that science dethrones man, but I suggest that the thrones that science can remove him from are those which he had no business occupying in the first place."

Donald M. MacKay
Science and the Quest for Meaning

"Modern Science therefore rejected the wrong thing: it separated itself from the idea of purpose in the universe."

Jacob Needleman
A Sense of the Cosmos, Pg. 36

"We cannot come to God except through prayer alone, for He is too high above us."

Martin Luther

"Darwin's theory is on the verge of collapse. He is in the process of being discarded, but perhaps in deference to the venerable old gentleman, resting comfortably in Westminster Abbey next to Sir Isaac Newton, it is being done as discreetly and gently as possible, with a minimum of publicity."

Attributed to biologist H. Smith *(Forgotten Truth)*

"Remarkably, modern Christian doctrine has moved a long way towards this picture of the integrated brain and mind, with its emphasis on the resurrection of the *whole man* through Christ."

Paul Davies
God and the New Physics, Pg. 96

Questions For Discussion

Chapter Six

1. Do you always find it easy to praise God, even in the midst of difficulties? Why or why not?

2. What are some "aids" to praise and gratitude? Do you use the Psalms, hymns, or other devotional aids when you pray?

3. List at least ten things we can praise God for every day. Is it difficult to find ten, or difficult to *stop* with ten? What does this say about *our* attitudes?

4. Do we tend to take our *blessings* for granted, but always remember to take our "complaints" to God? How do we feel when our children respond to us that way? How must God feel when we complain more than we praise or thank Him?

5. Are you more inclined to do favors for a child who is always appreciative and articulate in his or her thanks and gratitude? Do you think God is more ready to bless those who have consistently shown gratitude? Why or why not?

References

Prayer and Praise

Ezra 7:27-28
Psalms 8
Psalms 96
Psalms 100
Jeremiah 32:17-20
Daniel 6:10
Matthew 11:25
Luke 17:11-19
Acts 16:25
Romans 1:8
II Corinthians 6:10
Ephesians 5:20
Hebrews 13:15

Notes

Chapter Seven

Prayer and Healing

Is Jesus Still in the Healing Business?

Then saith He to the man, Stretch forth thy hand. And he stretched it forth and it was restored whole, like as the other.
Matthew 12:13

Both my pastor (and Carrie) always assured me that anything Jesus did when He was alive He was *still* doing through the power of the Comforter, His Holy Spirit. I wasn't sure I believed this, but began to think about it and to research the Scriptures to see what the Bible said about prayer and healing. Then one Sunday evening, close to Christmas, I had an opportunity to put it to the test.

I had begun to prepare a late dinner for my family. It was to be a simple supper, as was usual on a Sunday evening. I decided to fix scrambled eggs and link sausages–a favorite with the children.

101

I had a large electric griddle on which I arranged the sausages. The griddle had a trough around all four sides, to catch the grease as it accumulated. Before the sausages were done, I noticed the trough was nearly full to overflowing, so I removed the sausages and carried the griddle to the sink to pour off the grease.

As I tilted the griddle, I misjudged the angle and the hot grease poured all over my right hand (I am left-handed.) I screamed with the sudden pain. My husband, who was in the next room, came running. But before he got there, the entire palm of my hand had swelled up into one enormous blister. We could not even begin to get my ring off–the hand was so badly swollen.

At this stage of his career, my husband was the only plastic surgeon in our town or in the surrounding southwestern area of Michigan. He took care of all the burns from this area of over 500,000 people. Each month he saw many burn victims, and was responsible for their care. He knew burns to be the most painful injury a person can sustain.

One look at my hand and he said, "You have a third-degree burn which will probably require grafting in a week to ten days. I'll go to the hospital and get a burn dressing and some pain medication. I'll be back as soon as possible." He brought me a pan of snow to keep my hand in while he was gone. He then left for the hospital.

All of the children were crying and clinging to me in sympathy. Dinner was completely forgotten. When my husband returned, he examined the hand carefully and again pronounced it a third degree burn. All but the thumb and the end of the index finger were involved.

The burn treatment of choice at that time was to totally immobilize the affected area and wrap it snugly with the appropriate ointment and gauze bandages. My husband applied a splint to the hand and then a bulky dressing. By the time he finished, my hand looked as big as my head!

The reason for immobilizing the hand was to try to keep the blistered area from breaking open, thereby exposing the burned flesh to bacteria. He also cautioned me about getting the hand wet or soiled, which would also increase the chances of infection. He then gave me two empirin with codeine and put me to bed.

"In about four hours you'll wake up with pain again," he told me, "so I'm putting another two empirin here on your bedside table. When you wake up, take these. You'll be able to go back to sleep. Remember, don't get the dressing wet or dirty!"

The codeine soon took effect, and I drifted off to sleep. But at one o'clock in the morning I woke up with pain–just as my husband had said I would. I sat up on the edge of the bed and reached for the pills.

I thought to myself, "How does he expect me to keep my hand clean and dry? I have two babies in diapers, plus an eight year old to take care of!"

I recalled having recently read about Jesus restoring the withered hand of a man. (Matthew 12:13; Mark 3:1-5; Luke 6:6-10) Could He still heal damaged hands? If I asked in faith, believing He could do it, would He?

I sat there for a few moments, hesitating. I was afraid to ask for fear nothing would happen, and my meager faith would falter altogether. But what did I have to lose?

So I bowed my head and asked Jesus to heal my hand so that I could properly take care of my children. Immediately, the pain left me and all the swelling went out of my hand. The bandages drooped loosely. I knew the burn was completely gone; I was elated–then frightened. How would I explain it to my doubting husband? What would he say?

I sat there for a long time, trying to comprehend the immensity of what had happened. Why had my hand been healed, when none of my husband's patients had been? Many prayers had been offered on their behalf. I finally gave up trying to figure it out, and breathing a prayer of gratitude, lay back down and went to sleep.

My husband got up very early the next morning to make rounds, and did not awaken me or the children. When we woke up he was already gone. I asked Jeff to cut the dragging bandages off my hand. He refused.

"Oh, no," he said, "Daddy won't like that. He said to leave it alone."

At about 9:00 a.m. my sister drove up to spend the day with us. She lived in New York but, during the holidays, was visiting my parents in the neighboring city of Battle Creek.

I had her cut off the now both wet and soiled dressing. To my amazement the hand was perfectly normal! My sister, who at the time was not a Christian, couldn't believe the hand had ever been burned. But the boys all confirmed the fact that it had been severely blistered the night before. When I explained that prayer had healed the burn, Carolyn was as perplexed as they were. She had never heard of such a thing.

I was singing God's praises–grateful and relieved for the instantaneous healing! All morning long I kept looking at my hand, turning it over to stare at it in wonder and amazement. Now I couldn't wait to show it to my husband; he would have to admit to the power in prayer now–or so I thought.

He came home for lunch that day and did not notice or refer to my hand right away. But as I passed him a dish, he suddenly stiffened.

"Isn't that the hand you burned?" he demanded. "Where's the dressing I put on it?"

I turned the hand over for his inspection: "See," I said, "the burn is completely gone. I prayed that Jesus would heal it, and He did."

"I never heard anything so ridiculous in my life!" he shouted.

"But you can see for yourself. The hand is perfectly normal."

For a moment he glared at me, speechless; then he muttered under his breath, "I must have misdiagnosed it!"

But we both knew better.

The rest of the luncheon was very quiet. No one knew what to say. My husband quickly finished eating and left without even telling me good-bye. He was completely baffled.

That night after dinner, we both sat in the living room reading. He had a medical journal and I the Bible. I read again the account of Jesus healing the withered hand.

Then, putting the Bible down, I looked wonderingly at my own, now restored hand. What had happened? How had it come about?

If such healing is possible, why do so many people continue to suffer needlessly? Why had prayer worked for me?

Thinking of my husband's explanation ("I must have misdiagnosed it"), I said in a quiet voice, more to myself than to him, "Well, maybe you did **mis**-diagnose it."

Instantly he responded, "I never said that!"

That night we said no more about the matter. But from then on, my agnostic husband attended church regularly and began to study the Bible himself. (I thought about this remarkable event often and long.) Eventually, my husband suggested maybe I had just given myself a post-hypnotic suggestion. I remembered a hypnotist I had seen where he touched a hypnotized person's hand with a pencil (which he said was a cigarette), and a blister appeared on the hand. At the hypnotist's further suggestion, the blister immediately disappeared.

Had something similar occurred with me? Had I, in effect, given myself a post-hypnotic suggestion? Or was the healing of my hand truly an act of Jesus Christ in God?

Either solution was full of mystery; I could explain nothing. It was a miracle–no matter how I looked at it. But my mind would not let it rest, and in my attempts to understand how such an event might happen, I began to read widely in psychology.

In the meantime, I continued to study the Scriptures–and to pray.

That spring, my other sister and her husband (who were from Connecticut) came to visit. We had no guest room in our house, but our two younger boys shared a very large room in which we had installed twin trundle beds. I had pulled out the two trundles and pushed them together for my sister and brother-in-law.

In the morning Judy and I were making the beds together, talking and laughing as we worked. It was a beautiful, warm spring morning. I was barefoot.

As I made up one of the trundles and pushed it back under the twin bed, I failed to notice the trundle was not flush with the other bed. As I went around it, I caught my little toe on the projecting trundle. There was a loud, sharp CRACK!

"Ouch!" I shrieked, and looking down saw that my right little toe now stuck out at right angles to my foot!

My sister rushed to the telephone and called my husband, explaining what had happened. He was about to go into surgery so he couldn't come home to help us, but he told her I could either go to the emergency room to have it taken care of, or have Judy do it for me. He explained that all anyone could do was to put the toe back in its normal position and tape it to the next toe.

A cast could be put on to make it more comfortable when walking, but that wasn't really necessary. The important thing was to get the toe back into its normal position so it could heal.

So my sister and brother-in-law sat me down and one held me while the other snapped the crooked toe back and taped it in place. By this time the foot had begun to swell and there was a huge bruise spreading on the side of it. I spent the rest of the day with my foot elevated, while everyone waited on me.

By the time I went to bed that night the foot was enormous and the entire side of it was black from the blood seeping underneath the skin. It looked fright-ful–and felt worse!

As I lay there, I began to ponder. Prayer had worked on my burned hand. Could it also work on a broken toe?

Why not? According to the Bible, if I had faith enough, anything was possible! So before I fell asleep I prayed in the name of Jesus Christ that my foot would be healed by morning.

The next morning I awoke, and was halfway to the bathroom before I even remembered my broken toe. When I looked down the foot looked completely normal! All the swelling was gone and there wasn't a sign of the huge bruise which had covered half my foot the night before.

Tentatively I reached out and touched the "broken" toe. It was just slightly tender to the touch, but there was no pain when I walked.

I was "thunderstruck!" How could such things happen? This was the twentieth century; such miracles occurred during the first century. Could they still happen?

Why was this happening to me? What did it all mean? Why didn't such miraculous healings occur more often if prayer could bring about such miracles? Why did people continue to suffer needlessly? I wanted to know, to understand–but it was beyond my comprehension.

I knew of many people who had prayed for healing,but no healing occurred. Had I somehow triggered a response by some unconscious action or attitude?

My husband was inclined to believe this was likely the case. Somehow, under stress, he thought I must have activated some healing power within my organism which precipitated or speeded up the healing process and brought about the desired changes.

However, I gave the credit to God and praised Him for His healing power! His name is Wonderful! I continued to study the Scriptures earnestly in an effort to understand its mysteries.

I also continued to read in psychology and biology. And I continued to pray. By now I was fully convinced that Jesus still heals!

For Reflection

Prayer and Healing

"Fundamental physics is pointing the way to a new apppreciation of man and his place in the universe."

Paul Davies
God and the New Physics, Pg. vii

"At the personal level most people still find religious doctrine more persuasive than scientific arguments."

Ibid., Pg. 3

"When I seek thee, my God, I seek a blessed life."

St. Augustine

"As the mysterious linking of man with the Eternal, prayer is an incomprehensible wonder, a miracle of miracles which is daily brought to pass in the devout soul."

Friedrich Heiler
The Essence of Prayer

Questions for Discussion

Chapter Seven

1. Have you or someone you know ever experienced healing in response to prayer? Will you talk about it?

2. Has God ever answered, "No," to your request for healing? Has He ever said, "Not yet,"? Why doesn't He *always* heal when we pray in good faith? (More on this in Chapter 11: Unanswered Prayer.)

3. What is the relation of medicine to prayer? Should a Christian who has strong faith refuse medical help? Why or why not?

4. Why does God allow sickness and accidents at all? Can any good come from such suffering?

References

Prayer and Healing

Matthew 4:23-24
Matthew 8:1-17, 28-32
Matthew 9:1-8, 18-33
Matthew 15:21-28
Matthew 17:14-20
Matthew 20:29-34
Mark 1:21-32, 40-44
Mark 2:1-12
Mark 3:1-5
Mark 5:1-17, 21-43
Mark 7:25-37
Mark 8:22-25
Mark 9:14-29
Mark 10:46-52
Luke 4:38-41
Luke 6:6-10
Luke 9:37-43
Luke 13:10-13
Luke 17:12-19
Luke 18:35-43
John 4:46-54
John 5:1-9
John 9:1-7
John 11:38-44; 14:9-21; 15:1-26

Notes

Chapter Eight

Prayer and Our Relationships

Wherefore, I say unto thee, Her sins, which are many, are forgiven; for she loved much: but to whom little has been forgiven, the same loveth little.

Luke 7:47

Wherefore, laying aside all malice, and all guile, and hypocrisies, and envies, and all evil speakings, As newborn babes, desire the sincere milk of the word, that ye may grow thereby.

I Peter 2:1,2

But I say unto you, Love your enemies, bless them that curse you, do good to them that hate you, and pray for them which despitefully use you and persecute you.

Matthew 5:44

115

Before I became a Christian I knew very little about love–and many of my relationships showed it. I loved my husband when I got my own way, my son when he was obedient, and my parents, brothers and sisters (five of them) only if they didn't stay longer than three days.

Someone once told me that both "garbage and relatives stink after three days." Before I knew Jesus Christ, after three days I preferred the garbage to my own family.

This poor attitude showed itself when I was very young: "Your daughter deserves a medal which I duly will award her; alone her valiant efforts bring chaos out of order." Thus read the note my kindergarten teacher pinned to my blouse at the end of the first week of school.

My parents were not surprised by this message. They had spent five years trying to tame me. Just as in school, I was bringing chaos out of order at home.

And I continued in this manner–being a maelstrom of discontent and disorder, until I was thirty-five years old. Then I met *The Master.* I surrendered my life to Him, and from then on I have been *bringing order out of chaos.*

Within a week of my salvation, I *knew* something enormously significant had happened to me. I was *different.* Everything I heard, read, or thought about came out in *poetry.*

Robert Frost said a poet is one who brings "order out of chaos." Jesus Christ did that for me. He brought about a dramatic repentance. He literally turned me around–from being a master at bringing chaos out of order to one who, through the gift of His Holy (whole) Spirit, began to bring order out of chaos.

At the time of my salvation, I knew next to nothing about poetry *or* order. The only poet I had ever read was Walt Whitman, who had been assigned to me as my term paper topic in an English class.

I still know relatively little about poetry, but I can continue to write it because I now know a lot about Jesus Christ–no, *I know Him.*

This was not the only gift the Holy Spirit conferred upon me. Every aspect of my life began to exhibit a similar transformation.

Whereas, before I had no systematic schedule for *anything;* after my conversion housework was done regularly and routinely–and I learned to sing as I performed it. My home eventually became relatively clutter-free, dust-free, and resentment-free. (As a matter of fact, for a while I went overboard in the opposite direction, becoming "Super Mom!")

Laundry was done promptly, folded neatly, and put away immediately. Dirty dishes were no longer allowed to accumulate in the sink. There was a place for everything and everything went in its place.

Before I knew the Lord, I had a terrible (almost violent) temper. I was always "simmering" with anger at someone or something. That changed.

Shortly after my conversion, I was preparing Thanksgiving dinner for my entire extended family- about 17 people. The turkey was in the oven, nearly ready to carve, and there was a pot bubbling merrily on every burner of the stove-top.

I began to prepare the thickening for the gravy. I filled the gravy cup with water, added the proper amount of flour, put the top on the cup, and began to shake it vigorously. All of a sudden the top flew off and all that flour and water mixture sprayed all over the hot stove-it became instant glue-and my formerly coppertone colored range was suddenly white.

I stared at the mess I had created and burst into laughter as I realized how funny the stove and I, now coated with paste, looked! But my laughter stopped in amazement at my own reaction-a few days ago such an event would have filled me with rage. Now that Jesus was in my life, this misadventure seemed *humorous* rather than disastrous. I considered this a small miracle!

Since I started walking with Christ, my life has been one long series of small miracles. I *am becoming* an entirely new creation.

Sound too good to be true? That's what I used to think when those "pesky Christians" tried to persuade me to give Jesus a chance. Now I wish I had "capitulated" years earlier.

No, I'm not perfect yet, and neither are my loved ones–but we're on the way! Jesus has succeeded in straightening out most of the "kinks" a faulty gene pool (original sin) and a faulty upbringing has worked into all of us. For *all have sinned*, and each succeeding generation has contributed its parenting errors to the disaster.

A lifetime of psychotherapy could not do for us what Jesus does–and it is all *free* ! Available to anyone who accepts it.

Life has not been all bliss, but it has been *free of chaos*. Once their teaching value has been recognized, negative experiences have been welcomed. Seeing the world as a "school for souls" has put everything into its proper perspective.

When I first was told that, because Adam and Eve sinned, you and I would have to die, I thought, "What kind of crazy justice is that?" Then I realized that if death had not entered the world when sin did, we would still have among us such tyrants as Ghengis Kahn, Adolf Hitler, and Joseph Stalin–and we could never get rid of a Saddam Hussein!

Since such greedy, arrogant, selfish monsters don't care what they do to get their way, ordinary people like you and me would end up as their slaves, forced to do their bidding or suffer the consequences. And suffer we would, *interminably*, since death would never come for *any* of us. Endless torture would be the result for most of us. Death was God's *loving gift* to a humanity gone badly off track–going their *own way*, rather than *His way*.

But whoever will kneel at the foot of the cross, confessing their tendency to do everything "My Way," and accept Jesus Christ's sacrificial death in place of their own permanent death, will live forever in the heavenly kingdom with Him. Since no arrogant, greedy, self-centered person will kneel before anyone (even the King of Glory), there will be no arrogance or greed in Heaven.

Those greedy, arrogant, self-centered people will live forever too–with each other in eternal punishment. That's what will make it hell!

To enter the Heavenly Kingdom, we need God's forgiveness. We can never "earn" our way to Heaven. It is a gift–a gracious gift. It's *only* price is our acknowledgement of our neediness–*and our willingness to forgive others*.

Matthew 18:21-35 tells us that when we refuse to forgive others we cut off God's grace *to ourselves*. Jesus concludes this parable of the unmerciful servant by saying, *This is how my heavenly Father will treat each of you unless you forgive your brother from your heart.* (NIV)

And in His teaching of the disciples on prayer, He instructs them (and us) to pray *and forgive us our sins as we forgive those who sin against us.*

In Matthew 25:31-46, Jesus tells us . . . *whatever you did not do for one of the least of these, you did not do for me.* (NIV) Therefore, if we have been mean-spirited, vindictive, unforgiving, or self-centered concerning *anyone*, the Lord says that's how we've treated Him and His Holy Spirit.

He tells us, "The greatest commandment is to love the Lord your God with all your heart, soul, and mind . . . ." And the second is like it: "love your neighbor as yourself."

As we learn in John 14, we are to love *as God loves.* Refusing to love as He loves is to refuse the ministry of the Holy Spirit.

Matthew Seven contains some of the most important instructions on relationships in the Bible. Jesus warns us, *Do not judge, or you too will be judged.* And beginning with verse 21 we read these words: *Not everyone who says to me 'Lord, Lord' will enter the kingdom of heaven, but only he who does the will of my Father who is in heaven. Many will say to me on that day, 'Lord, Lord, did we not prophesy in your name, and in your name drive out demons and perform many miracles?' Then I will tell them plainly, 'I never knew you. Away from me, you evildoers!'* (NIV)

These words must be taken seriously. Whenever we judge *anyone*-including our own family members-we are in danger of bringing judgment upon ourselves.

This does not mean we are not to discipline our children. But we are to discipline *in love*. Instead of coercing or threatening our loved ones, we are to treat them with loving kindness and patience.

When my children were small, I learned an important lesson. Because I am a morning person, I would go rushing into my sons' bedrooms, yank the blinds up with a snap, pull down the bedclothes, and cheerfully announce, "Rise and shine–time to get up, up, and at 'em!" Needless to say, my family did *not* welcome the dawn as enthusiastically as I did, and I was faced with three grumpy boys at the breakfast table.

Finally, one morning my husband said to me, "Let me try waking them up for a change."

He tip-toed into their rooms, leaned close to their still-sleeping heads, and whispered, "It's almost time to get up. Why don't you start waking up now. I'll go shave and come back in a few minutes to be sure you're awake."

Five minutes later, he again quietly and gently reminded them it was time to get up. The third time he went in he would *quietly* raise the shade, give them another hug, and remind them breakfast was almost ready.

Amazingly, the morning atmosphere began to change. I learned from this and other incidents that "you can catch more flies with honey than you can with vinegar." I wasn't *using* vinegar, but I had not been as considerate as my husband was.

Little by little Christ worked on my disposition, personality, and character–He's still working on it. If there is anyone in the Kingdom of Heaven for whom our presence there would make it seem like Hell, we may not get in. Jesus tells us, *Be ye perfect, even as your Heavenly Father is perfect.* (Matthew 5:48) Only gracious, loving people will be admitted to Heaven–again, that's what will make it Heaven. We must all become like Jesus, full of gracious love.

The difference between the Kingdoms of Heaven and Hell are illustrated by this story:

A fine Christian man died suddenly, and immediately found himself before St. Peter at the pearly gates. Peter greeted him warmly, telling him that he was expected, but before the man could enter Heaven he was required to take a tour of Hell–so he would know what he had missed and thus appreciate Heaven. St. Peter would accompany him.

They walked down a long spiral staircase to a huge steel door marked, "Hell. No admittance without proper identification." Peter knocked and Satan promptly opened the door.

"Satan, we're here for the usual tour."

"Of course," responded the devil, "Come right in and make yourselves at home."

As they walked in, the recently deceased Christian looked around him in wide-eyed disbelief. The Kingdom of Hell was beautiful. It looked like an extension of Florida's Cypress Gardens. There were beautifully manicured lawns, gorgeous flower beds, magnificent flowering shrubs and trees, and the golden crystal walk on which they were standing wound gently up to a marvelous building more impressive than the most recent Hyatt Regency Hotel.

"Wow," he thought to himself. "If this is Hell, I can't *wait* to see what Heaven is like!"

"We're just in time for lunch," announced Peter. "Let's go join them in the dining room. I think that's all we'll need to see. Then we can go back to Heaven."

Our friend dutifully followed St. Peter up to the building and into the magnificent dining room. Looking around, he saw long tables set with beautiful snowy damask cloths, golden candelabra, and golden plates with gorgeous arrangements of fruits, meats, and sweets in the center of each table.

At the sound of a gong, people began streaming into the room, taking their seats at the tables. As Peter pulled out a chair for him, our Christian friend noticed there was no cutlery on the tables. How were they to eat without knives, forks, or spoons? Just then another gong sounded and out from the kitchen came regally suited waiters carrying trays of cutlery–all four feet long.

Each diner was given a set of these over-sized utensils and they began to try to eat with them. But the long handles made it extremely difficult. They could hardly maneuver them to their mouths, and the long handles jabbed their neighbors repeatedly.

Soon everyone was angrily accusing his neighbor of intruding on his space. They began to scuffle and then to fight. Hitting one another over the head with their enormous spoons and forks, jabbing one another, throwing food at each other. It was total chaos, worse than any dorm food-fight ever seen on earth.

After a few minutes, St. Peter took the Christian by the arm.

"I think we've seen enough," he chuckled. "Why don't we go back to Heaven. If we hurry we can still get lunch upstairs."

So back they went, up the spiral staircase to the pearly gates. But when St. Peter pushed them open the man was astonished to see exactly the same landscape he had witnessed below.

"What's going on?" he wondered. "Heaven doesn't look any different than Hell."

They hurried up to the gorgeous Hyatt-like building and into the dining room. All was just as it had been in Hell. The waiters were just bringing in the cutlery-all of it four feet long.

But as each resident received his knife, fork, and spoon, they quietly bowed in prayer, and after saying grace, picked up their silverware and began to feed the person across the table from them–the difference between Heaven and Hell.

For Reflection

Prayer and Our Relationships

"Every human, both saint and sinner, is an expression of God. No matter how distorted the manifestation may be, that person is a fragment of the divine. The Bible tells us that to fail to love that person is failure to love God."

Cecil Osborne
The Joy of Understanding Your Faith

"Contrary to Mrs. Grundy, sex is not sin. Contrary to Hugh Hefner, it's not salvation either. Like nitroglycerin, it can be used either to blow up bridges or to heal hearts."

Frederick Beuchner
Wishful Thinking

Questions for Discussion

Chapter Eight

1. How good are you at forgiving? Is there any Christian whose presence you could not tolerate for eternity? Is there any brother or sister who could not tolerate *your* presence for eternity? What would the Lord want you to do about this situation?

2. How are you at *forgetting* once you have forgiven? If we don't forget, have we *really forgiven? Ask the Lord to help you to forget as well as to forgive!*

3. How many times are we to forgive our brothers and sisters?

4. If you have offended anyone (*especially* among your own family!) can you go to them and ask forgiveness? What would Jesus tell us to do?

References

Prayer and Our Relationships

Deuteronomy 32:35
Proverbs 21:19
Proverbs 28:9
Ezekiel 18:21-22
Matthew 5:22-24, 38-44
Matthew 6:14-15
Matthew 7:1-5, 12-14
Matthew 8:21-22
Matthew 9:9-13
Matthew 10:34-42
Matthew 11:29
Matthew 12:7-25, 46-50
Matthew 18:15-35
Matthew 19:13-14
Matthew 22:37-39
Matthew 23:11-13
Mark 11:25-26
Luke 11:4
I Corinthians 13
Ephesians 5:1-33, 6:1-9
Colossians 3:18-25
I John 3
I Peter 3:1-17

Notes

Chapter Nine

Prayer
and the Holy Spirit

What is the Role of the Holy Spirit
in an Effective Prayer Life?

*Know ye not that ye are the temple of God,
and that the Spirit of God dwelleth in you?"*
I Cor. 3:16

Occasionally someone will ask me, "Do you have the
Holy Spirit? Can you speak in tongues?"

Frankly, I don't think anyone can *have* the Holy
Spirit. But I know the Holy Spirit *can have us!* I
believe we each need a fresh anointing of the Spirit
every day. I learned this important lesson when my
youngest child was about eight months old.

It is especially hard to learn a new skill in a "fox-
hole"–but that's where I first became very serious

131

about prayer and learned what being *filled with the Spirit* was like.

Perhaps you, too, first took prayer seriously when you were faced with a crisis. Although most of us probably say grace before meals and pray before falling asleep at night, these prayers often become standardized and can be repeated almost by rote. What I learned in my foxhole was what I now call "soaking prayer."

Soaking prayer requires time. Quality time. *Sacrificial time.* By that I mean we must give up doing something else we would like to do. For some it may be watching television, playing golf, tennis, or bridge, talking on the telephone, or reading novels–for me it was sleep.

When my third child was born with a severe birth defect, my stamina was challenged as never before. Brian had to wear full leg casts from the day of birth until he was over a year old. He was naturally a light and restless sleeper; the casts further complicated the situation.

Whenever he tried to turn over or change position, the weight of the casts would awaken him. He rarely slept for more than twenty to thirty minutes at a time. When awakened he would cry, thereby waking me, too. So neither of us ever got enough sleep.

As the months went by, I became progressively more exhausted. The more tired I became, the more depressed I felt. I could not nap during the day because the other two boys required my supervision–even if the baby had fallen asleep.

I stopped "trying" to get to church. Getting myself and three little ones ready proved too great a challenge for my diminished energies. However, I did maintain daily devotions.

One morning my Scripture reading was Isaiah 40:29-31 (LB). *He gives power to the tired and worn out, and strength to the weak. Even the youths shall be exhausted, and the young men will all give up. But they who wait upon the Lord shall renew their strength; they shall mount up with wings like eagles; they shall run and not be weary; they shall walk and not faint.*

These verses leaped off the page at me. But what did it mean to "wait upon the Lord?" I pondered this all day long.

Late that afternoon my mother called to ask if I was planning on cooking Thanksgiving dinner that year. It was my turn. I told her we were cancelling Thanksgiving because I was too tired to even eat it, much less cook it. The holiday was thirty-two days away. She said if I didn't feel up to it in November, she would be glad to prepare the meal.

That evening I re-read Isaiah 40:31. I still didn't understand exactly how one *waited upon the Lord*, but I decided I was going to try it to see if God would *restore my strength.*

I resolved to spend one hour every morning waiting on God. To do this I had to get up at 5:45. Of course it made no sense to get up an hour earlier when what I suffered was from too little sleep. But I was desperate enough to try it. I vowed to continue this "waiting" for thirty days. If my vitality didn't increase I would give it up.

So the next morning I rose at 5:45 and put Brian in our bed, telling my husband he was on duty for the next sixty minutes.

Our living room had a huge picture window on the east wall. With Bible in hand, I sat on the stair landing and looked out that window at the still dark, sleeping world. As I watched I recited Psalms 100 and 103, then the critical passage in Isaiah. I asked God to come into my life in such a powerful way that my strength would be *renewed like the eagles*, so I, too, could *run, and not be weary; . . . walk and not faint.* (Isaiah 40:31)

That first morning nothing unusual happened, but I *did* enjoy the peace and quiet of an hour alone with God. It was beautifully still until the sun came up and summoned the birds from their slumber. As I watched and listened, it was as though the birds were singing *Morning Has Broken*. I decided to keep my appointment with God the next day, too, just for the sheer enjoyment of the stillness and the dawn's beauty.

For twenty-nine consecutive mornings I sat and greeted God and the new day. It was pleasant, but I grew progressively more exhausted. I was relieved as I struggled out of bed at 5:45 on the thirtieth day for what was, I thought, the last time.

But this morning proved to be very different from the previous twenty-nine. I sat as usual, praying and praising God, watching the horizon brighten. As the rim of the sun appeared I began to feel a warmth spread throughout my entire body. Simultaneously, I was filled with joy. An elation, like nothing I had ever experienced, overwhelmed me. Suddenly, I was bursting with energy.

This strength never abated. I called my mother that day and told her I would cook Thanksgiving dinner. At the end of that day I was still going strong.

Brian continued to be a restless sleeper, and I unfailingly rose an hour early to wait upon the Lord for several more months. But eventually his problems were corrected, the casts removed, and he began to sleep more normally.

As long as I arose and spent that first hour with God, my energy seemed inexhaustible. When I stopped getting up at 5:45 my energy slowly dwindled. Recognizing what had happened, I re-established that precious hour. I still spend the first hour of the day waiting upon the King of Glory. He never disappoints me. He is always there, waiting for me. Each day He fills me with His Holy Spirit, giving just enough Grace for the day.

The Church seems to fall into one of two errors concerning the Holy Spirit. Either we make *too little* of the third person of the trinity, scarcely acknowledging His existence, or we make *too much* of Him, ignoring the first two persons.

Jesus makes it clear in John 14 that the "Comforter" or "Counsellor" would not come unless He (Jesus) returned to His Father. And in the first chapter of Acts we learn that after His resurrection when He appeared to the disciples He instructed them not to leave Jerusalem until they received the gift of the Holy Spirit, telling them, ...*you will receive power when the Holy Spirit comes on you; and you will be my witnesses in Jerusalem, and in all Judea and Samaria, and to the ends of the earth.* (Acts 1:8 NIV)

After Pentecost these formerly subdued, defeated disciples suddenly leap off the pages of the New Testament, filled with the supernatural power of the Holy Spirit! *We* must be similarly empowered! In churches where the Holy Spirit is ignored you rarely find much vitality. Such congregations seem to plod along, but rarely "set the world on fire for Jesus."

On the other hand, in some denominations which over-emphasize baptism in the Holy Spirit, we sometimes see exaggerated, out-of-balance emotionalism running rampant.

Perhaps it is better to err on the side of over-concentration on the Holy Spirit than to err by too little concern for Him. For the Holy Spirit is a person and He is *the* person to whom we have the most intimate relationship at this stage of Christ's Church.

God the Father is in Heaven; Jesus the Son is now in Heaven with the Father; only the Holy Spirit is presently here on earth. He is our empowerment today just as He was for the disciples following Pentecost.

Our body is the temple of the Holy Spirit. We grieve or quench the Holy Spirit when we refuse to make a home for Him in our bodies, in our own spirits, in our lives. Unless we seek Him out daily we may have to function without Him.

I know I can't function very well or very long without His constant re-filling and daily baptism.

Remember, *Your heavenly Father (will) give the Holy Spirit to them that ask for Him.* (Luke 11:13) Have you asked? What have you asked of God that requires supernatural power? That which would be impossible without the empowering of the Holy Spirit.

For Reflection

Prayer and the Holy Spirit

"Prayer then becomes the growing edge of the spirit, the point at which we use concentration, sensitivity, and self-understanding to grow beyond our prejudices, fears, and immature emotional traits."

Edgar Jackson
Understanding Prayer, Pg. 47

"The miracle of prayer does not lie in the accomplishment of the prayer, of the influence of man on God, but in the mysterious contact which comes to pass between the finite and the infinite Spirit."

Friedrich Heiler
The Essence of Prayer

"The meaning of earthly existence lies, not as we have grown used to thinking, in prospering, but in the development of the soul."

Alexander Solzhenitsyn
As quoted by Charles Colson, *Loving God*

"Oh Christian, take time each day to receive from the Father the continual guidance of the Holy Spirit. Let Him overcome the world for you, and strengthen you as a child of heaven to walk daily with your God and with the Lord Jesus . . . The Holy Spirit will do His part if you in faith surrender yourself to His control. You will learn to speak to others with such heavenly joy that you will draw them to give themselves to the Holy Spirit and walk in the joy of Christ's love."

Charles G. Finney
The Believer's Secret of Spiritual Power, Pg. 134.

"Two prisoners in contingent cells communicate by blows struck on the wall. The wall is what separates them, but also what permits them to communicate. So it is with us and God. Every separation is a bond."

Simone Weil
As quoted by May Sarton, *The Small Room*

"This does not mean that God stands idly by and allows us to flounder in the misery of our own making. The troubles that man brings upon himself allow God to demonstrate His love for us. "

Russell Stannard
Science and the Renewal of Belief

Questions for Discussion

Chapter Nine

1. Do you think your church places enough emphasis on the work of the Holy Spirit? Why or why not?

2. Have you personally experienced the baptism of the Holy Spirit? Do you think *all* Christians are "automatically" filled with the Spirit? Do you agree that we all need to seek a fresh infilling daily?

3. What are some things you or your congregation have experienced as a result of Holy Spirit activity?

4. What do you think Satan wants us to believe about the Holy Spirit?

References

Prayer and the Holy Spirit

Isaiah 59:21
Luke 11:13
John 16:13-15
Romans 8:9-18, 26-27
I Corinthians 6:19-20
I Corinthians 12:1-13
Galatians 5:5, 22-26
Ephesians 1:16-17
Ephesians 4:30
Ephesians 5:18
Ephesians 6:17-18
I Thessalonians 5:19
I John 3:24
I John 4:1-13
Jude 1:17-23

Notes

Chapter Ten

Intercessory Prayer

"Standing in the Gap"
for a Suffering Humanity

. . . The prayer of faith shall save the sick, and the Lord shall raise him up; and if he have committed sins, they shall be forgiven him.

James 5:15

Likewise the Spirit also helpeth our infirmities: for we know not what we should pray for as we ought: but the Spirit itself maketh intercession for us with groanings which cannot be uttered. And he that searcheth the hearts knoweth what is the mind of the Spirit, because he maketh intercession for the saints according to the will of God.

Romans 8:26, 27

When I first became a believer and started my prayer "experiments," I usually prayed for myself and my family. I had so many personal needs that I couldn't see beyond my own extended family. Consequently, I did not become sensitive to the needs of others, until the time when my children were in school. But little by little the Lord turned me from my absorbtion with my own loved ones, to concerns for my neighbors, my community, and the world at large.

Perhaps I was more in need of personal growth and transformation because I had not grown up in the Church. **When you have no god to set your standards and practices, it is very easy to become your own god.** I was like many other humanistic atheists–very self-absorbed; I worshipped myself and my own puny intellect.

But once I acknowledged the Lordship of Christ, I began to change. Slowly I became an intercessor, praying for people I did not know. My parents and brothers and sisters could not believe it when they heard that I was volunteering to work at the Kalamazoo Deacons Conference, the Michigan Rehabilitation Center for the Blind, the County Jail, the Gospel Mission, and the Corrections Center–I could scarcely believe it myself.

But as I struggled to bring my life into conformity with the commandments of Jesus, the Holy Spirit was working in me to fulfill the promise, *Therefore if any man be in Christ, he is a new creature: old things are*

passed away; behold, all things are become new.
(II Corinthians 5:17)

I was indeed becoming a new creature. The most significant change was the change in my inner attitude. Before I knew Christ I had little love to share; I loved only those who could meet *my* needs. Since becoming a Christian, I had begun to grow in love. I began to reach out to people in a caring way, wanting to be able to meet *their* needs.

I experienced long periods of utter peace and quiet joy. To be sure, there were still times when the peace and joy were absent–but those times became shorter and less frequent. And I began to discern a pattern to their coming and going.

When I was faithful to God's Word, I experienced the peace *that passes understanding;* when I fell away from His Word, I became restless and ill at ease. The closer I stayed to Jesus Christ, the closer the HolySpirit pulled me to God and to the fruits of the Spirit: love, peace, joy, patience, kindness, goodness, faithfulness, gentleness, and self-control. More and more I have become convinced that the Scriptures truly hold the key to successful living–they are the Words of Life–just as Jesus' disciples said.

Both my husband and I had studied psychology and worked in the field–he as a psychiatrist in the Navy, I as a Mental Health Education Specialist and Guidance Counselor. With my husband's renewed interest in the Bible, we spent much time discussing various psychiatric theories and practices, comparing them with Scriptural approaches, struggling to understand prayer, why it seems to work sometimes and not others. Was God merely "whimsical," or are there good reasons why some prayers are answered, "No," or "Not yet," while others receive prompt, affirmative answers? Is it God's will to say no, or are there other factors at work when prayers are answered in the negative-or not at all? Because of his medical training (or his weaker faith), my husband believed that many of my answered prayers were activities in the psyche which had the desired effect on the body. In order to convince him otherwise, I kept looking for something to pray about which my psyche could not possibly effect or interfere with.

I found it one day in mid July, when our boys were still very small.

When we had moved into our house, there were five beautiful American elm trees in our front yard. One by one they had become diseased and had to be taken down. Finally, in July my husband called to have men come to take down the last two trees.

One of the trees was my favorite. It was in the front of the house and shaded our living room, dining room, and bedroom. On summer nights I could hear its leaves rustling just outside my bedroom window. In winter its graceful branches made a lovely design against the sky. I was sad to lose that tree.

As it happened, on the morning the men came to cut down the two trees, I had read the Biblical account of Jesus cursing the fig tree (Matt. 21:19). Then, I began to speculate: if Jesus could kill a tree with a word, could He not heal a dead tree? Here was something my psyche certainly had no control over. If I prayed for the tree and it revived, my husband surely couldn't contend that *I* had somehow "subconsciously" influenced the results.

So I approached the tree expert and asked him to leave the only remaining tree standing.

"Lady," he said, "If I have to make another trip out here with all this equipment it's going to cost you additional money. You better let me take it down now. The Doc won't like it if he comes home and sees I only did half the job he told me to do."

"I'll take full responsibility," I assured him. "I'm not ready to lose that tree."

Shaking his head in perplexity, he called off his men and began loading his equipment.

"Okay, Lady," he mumbled, "but you be sure to tell the Doc this was *your* idea, not mine!"

After he had gone, I began to regret my hasty decision. But calling my three little boys to me, I explained that we were going to try an "experiment." "Every day all four of us are going to pray for that tree," I said.

We would see whether prayer could influence an already dead tree. I read them the Biblical account of

Jesus raising Lazarus from the dead (John 11) and also the account of His cursing the fig tree.

Because they were so young, and had the faith of little children, they saw nothing remarkable in this idea. However, Jeff, the oldest, remarked, "I don't think Daddy is going to understand."

What an understatement.

I have never come closer to divorce than I did that night. My husband was sure I had completely flipped. That tree was dead–it was too late for prayer or anything else. I would have to pay for the tree removal myself.

In spite of my husband's protests, the children and I continued to pray for the elm tree. Each time we passed it we would pause, lay our hands on the trunk, and breathe a prayer for its revival.

All winter long, as I watched the sun rise behind the beautiful tracery of its graceful branches, I prayed that God would honor our prayers for its survival, and thus glorify His Holy Name.

As the months passed, my faith in the Lord's ability and intent grew. I was sure He had heard our prayers and they would be answered affirmatively. The boys too, were certain God would not deny our request.

When April came the elm tree filled out in full leaf! It appeared to be completely healthy again. Only my husband was surprised, and "flabbergasted." The boys and I laughed and praised the Lord. Is anything too hard for God?

Interestingly enough, there is more to the story about the elm tree. Out of habit, I continued to say a prayer for that tree every time I looked at it, and it remained healthy and beautiful. Several years later we moved to a larger house and I bade the tree a sad farewell.

We had moved in late April. About six weeks later, one of my former neighbors called and invited me for coffee. As I drove past our former home I was stunned to see that the elm was completely dead; no one was praying for it anymore. A month later the new owners had it removed.

My husband could not argue with our success. He responded by increasing his Bible study and church attendance. He was now attending both morning and evening services, plus mid-week Bible study. He had stopped vehemently disputing the power of prayer.

Our new home had a beautiful, large yard with many oak trees in the rear. It was an all-brick walk-out ranch style house. I wasn't as impressed with the house as I was with the yard; I loved all the oak trees which shaded the patio area and provided a natural screen between our yard and the neighbors.

On July 4th, we invited my two brothers and their families for a back-yard barbecue. It was a beautiful day with azure skies and a gentle breeze. When we had finished eating, we continued to lounge on the patio, enjoying the lovely summer afternoon.

Suddenly, my oldest brother, who had been relaxing on the chaise, sat bolt upright and, pointing into the woods, said, "Nancy, what's wrong with that tree?"

We all looked where he was pointing. All of the leaves on one of the oaks were completely wilted.

"I don't know what's wrong with it, John. Maybe it doesn't get enough water," I responded. (We live in a swamp, that was the only reason I could think of.)

My husband went over to examine the tree more closely.

"You'd better call the tree people tomorrow and ask them to take a look at it. It doesn't look right at all," he told me. "Call the county extension agent, too, for a second opinion."

So the next day (Tuesday) I called and made arrangements for the two experts to come look at the tree on Wednesday morning.

Within an hour of one another, the men came and examined the tree. Then they left the same dismal diagnosis: *Oak Wilt.*

Both said there had been several cases of this dreaded tree disease in the county already–and there was nothing we could do to cure it or prevent its spread.

Oak Wilt is a fungus spread through the root system of the trees. Since the roots of our oaks were all intermingled underground, they would all eventually succumb as the fungus attacked their roots. The best thing to do would be to chop all the trees down and wait for the fungus to die off in four to five years or so, then plant new trees.

Their prognoses devastated me. I loved the yard because of all the beautiful trees. It would take fifty years to grow new mature trees.

As I was standing in the dining room looking out at the obviously dying tree, Brian came into the room.

"What's wrong, Mom? You look so sad." he said.

"Oh, Brian, the tree men said we will lose all our trees. That sick one has Oak Wilt and there's no way to cure it or to stop it from spreading to the other oaks. We'll lose them *all!*" I wailed.

"No we won't, Mom!" Brian said. "Let's pray for it, just like we did for that tree at the old house. God can heal it and keep the other trees healthy too."

So right then and there we dropped to our knees and asked the Lord to restore our oak trees.

The next Sunday when we had come home from church, I went into the kitchen to prepare dinner while my husband and the two younger boys set the table in the dining room.

Suddenly I heard my husband shout, "Nancy, come in here and look at this tree!"

I rushed into the dining room to see what his excitement was about. To my astonishment, the infected tree had shed all its wilted leaves *and* had grown brand new baby leaves. That was the last we saw of Oak Wilt.

The entire family was inspired by this answer to prayer, and I began to spend even more time in intercessory prayer.

I also went back to studying the Scriptures with renewed enthusiasm. As a young Christian, I had a tendency to view the Bible as a mysterious collection of esoteric wisdom–something requiring great insight and persistence in order to understand all the "symbolism" contained in it. But a mature Christian friend suggested that I try to accept the Bible at face value, taking each command and promise as a simple, easy to understand message instructing me how to live the Christian life.

She did not deny that there may be some profound symbolism in the Scriptures. She pointed out that I did not have to *understand* the principles it contained–I needed only "OBEY THEM." No amount of esoteric insight will unlock the spiritual power of God's Word. But even the smallest attempt to believe and obey God brings immediate results in our lives.

One of the biggest stumbling blocks to my own spiritual growth was pride. I thought I would have to understand God and His Word before I surrendered my will to Him.

The more I studied the Bible, the more my respect for its contents continued to grow. Yet there were passages which utterly perplexed me. For example, *Ask anything in my name, and I will do it.* (John 14:12-13 Paraphrased)

I asked myself, why do people still suffer and die, in spite of sincere prayers and devout living? If God is who He claims to be, and the Scriptures accurate records of His instructions, what is wrong?

Hoping to find an explanation, I continued to read everything I could find on prayer. Praying for insight and wisdom, I continued to pore over the Scriptures.

As my times of prayer became longer and more intense, I became more sensitive to God's "still, small voice," and learned to listen attentively for His leading.

By this time I had become a member of Christian Women's Club and was serving as Area Representative, giving direction and assistance to the three clubs in our community. One day I invited the immediate past-chairmen and the incoming chairmen to my home for lunch, in order to discuss the imminent change of officers.

After we had eaten and made the necessary arrangements for the change in leadership, one of the women turned to me and said, "Nancy, would you put one of our members on your prayer list? She's in a coma in the hospital and not expected to live. She was hospitalized ten days ago, suffering from severe rheumatoid arthritis and convulsions. Her heart has stopped several times and she's in *intensive care* with a special duty nurse around the clock. We're very concerned about her. She has several small children at home who need their mother."

"Of course I'll pray for her." I responded. "I'll put her name at the top of my list."

By this time I had a very extensive list of prayer requests, but I did put the desperately ill young mother at the top of it.

The next morning, while I was praying for her, I sensed the Lord was telling me to go visit this young mother.

"All right, Lord. I'll go as soon as I finish my prayers and do my housework," I told Him.

"No. Go now. *Right now!*" He seemed to say. So I got up, dressed, got in my car, and drove to the hospital.

When I entered her room I found her in an oxygen tent with electrodes connected to her head, chest, wrists, and feet as an electrical monitor recorded her heart rate, electrical brain activity, and other vital signs. The special duty nurse at her side watched as her patient inhaled and exhaled, alert to any change in her breathing.

I greeted the nurse and stood for a moment, trying to decide what to do next.

"Can she hear me if I speak to her?" I asked the nurse.

"There's no way to tell," was her response. "When they come out of a coma some patients report having heard everything that went on; others seem to have been totally out of it. It certainly won't do any harm to speak to her. Who knows? It might do some good–only time will tell."

So I moved to the head of her bed, opposite the nurse, and knelt down so my mouth was about at her ear level. I spoke in a soft voice.

"I know you don't know who I am, but your friends from Christian Women's Club asked me to pray for you. While I was praying this morning the Lord told me to come pray for you. He wants you to know how much He loves you. We are all praying for you and your family–for your complete recovery, and for courage and faith for your loved ones. They need you and we do, too. We're praying you'll be able to leave the hospital and resume your family duties, and attend Christian Women's Club again."

I continued to pray quietly until I could think of nothing else to say. The patient showed no signs of consciousness. Finally, I rose to my feet and started to turn away. Then I thought I heard her say, "I need mothering."

I turned back quickly, but saw no change, and the nurse did not appear to have heard anything. Was my mind playing tricks on me? Had she spoken? Or was it the Holy Spirit speaking?

I returned to my kneeling position next to her head.

"Well, if you need mothering, that must be the reason God sent me to you. *I* need a daughter. Let's team up! If you'll get well, I'll be delighted to be a mother to you and you can become a daughter to me. I'll be back tomorrow, dear."

On my way home I stopped at a nearby florist and had a pink rose in a bud vase with a balloon attached sent and signed the card, "Your new Mother."

The next day I again drove to the hospital, arriving about 10:00 a.m. When I walked into her room I stopped short–astonished by what I saw.

She was sitting up in bed, eating from a breakfast tray, watching "I Love Lucy" and laughing heartily. On her bedside stand was the rose and balloon.

I introduced myself and asked if she recalled my previous visit. She remembered nothing. The nurse explained that when the florist had delivered the rose she had read the enclosed card aloud to the patient.

There had been no immediate change, but about a half hour later the patient began to show signs of consciousness. By evening she was fully conscious, sitting up and asking for something to eat. She had slept soundly, and naturally, all night, awakening about nine o'clock and again requested food.

As we talked, I learned her tragic story. She had been one of four little girls whose parents divorced shortly after the birth of the youngest daughter. Although the mother was an alcoholic, the state had awarded her custody of the children, because in those days the mother *always* got to keep the children.

However, this mother was unable to tolerate such demanding responsibility, and when the patient was four years old she abandoned them in a farmhouse in the middle of winter. After two days, the furnace went out and they had no food left. The oldest girl called the telephone operator and asked if she could send them some food and someone to build a fire. The operator had the good sense to keep the child on the line while they traced the call, and within the hour the Sheriff's Department sent a car to pick up the cold, hungry children.

The mother was untraceable, but the Department of Social Services located the father, who had since remarried a woman with four children of her own. They had had another child and were understandably not eager to take on four more. But there was no choice, and the four little girls moved into an already crowded three bedroom, one bath house.

The new stepmother tried to be a mother to all nine children, but had little time to do anything but cook, clean, and do laundry. As a result, our patient received very little mothering from then on–and had received very little before then. So I became a surrogate mother to her.

It was easy to "mother" her. She was a beautiful, talented, spirited young woman, a daughter any mother would have been proud of.

By the end of the month she was well enough to accompany me when I went out of town to speak. She had a beautiful soprano voice, and began to sing for the groups to which I spoke.

Eventually, she began to give her own testimony, and for about three years we travelled together, speaking and singing as a team. Our partnership was interrupted when I was diagnosed with breast cancer (more about this in a later chapter.)

This daughter's healing had been the first dramatic answer of intercessory prayer I'd experienced–but not the last. Over the years the Lord has graciously answered many of my prayers for others.

Remember, we are *supposed* to become God's errand runners–His hands, feet, eyes, and ears. Many (including myself) start out expecting God to become our "celestial errand boy," but if we are growing spiritually, we begin to realize it is *we* who are supposed to serve *Him*. Gradually, we make ourselves available to do His bidding.

Perhaps one of the reasons some prayers take so long to be answered is because there are so few people taking their orders from "headquarters." God depends on *us* to help Him meet the needs of the world. In order to do so we must learn to *listen to God* instead of always telling im what we want Him to do for us. Intercessors are necessary for the coming of the Kingdom.

For Reflection

Intercessory Prayer

"The Church is the only cooperative society in the world that exists for the benefit of its non-members."

Archbishop of Canterbury & Wm. Temple
As quoted by Charles Colson, *Loving God*

"But we will only be weak and stumbling believers and a crippled church unless and until we truly apply God's Word–that is, until we truly love Him and act on that love."

Charles Colson
Loving God

"There is nothing more powerful than prayer."

Chrysostom

Questions for Discussion

Chapter Ten

1. Have you seen answers to your prayers of intercession? Can you talk about it?

2. How extensive should our prayer list be? Should we pray for local, state, national, and international authorities?

3. Do our pastors need our prayers of intercession?

4. What areas of our world especially need prayers of intercession?

References

Intercessory Prayer

Genesis 20:17
Numbers 21:7
II Chronicles 7:14
Matthew 5:44
Luke 18:1
Acts 1:14
Romans 8:26
II Corinthians 5:20
II Thessalonians 1:11
II Thessalonians 3:1
Hebrews 13:18
I Timothy 2:8
James 5:13-16

Notes

Chapter Eleven

Unanswered Prayer

Happiness or Holiness?
Why God Says, "No," or "Not Yet,"
to Some of Our Requests.

*For I was hungry and you wouldn't feed Me,
thirsty, and you wouldn't give Me anything to
drink; A stranger, and you refused me hospitality;*
Matthew 25:42 (LB)

*If I regard iniquity in my heart, the Lord will
not hear me.*
Psalms 66:18

You cannot serve two masters; God and money.
Matthew 6:24 (LB)

*. . . ye have not, because ye ask not. Ye ask,
and receive not, because ye ask amiss . . . .*
James 4:2

163

*You husbands must be careful of your wives,
being thoughtful of their needs and honoring
them as the weaker sex; remember that you and
your wife are partners in receiving God's blessings together and if you don't treat her as you
should, your prayers will not get ready answers.*
I Peter 3:7 (LB)

Whenever I speak to a group about prayer, someone
will ask, "Why hasn't God answered *my* prayers?"
Often they sound hurt, resentful, or just plain baffled.
Why doesn't God answer all our prayers as we want
Him to?

Christians who ponder it usually come up with the
same answer: God doesn't grant all our requests for
the same reason we don't grant all of *our* children's
requests: some of the requests we make are not really
in our best interest in the long run.

I suspect there is more to both the question and
answer than we sometimes realize. I don't know about
you, but I rarely grow until I become so uncomfortable
I am forced to change. In order to bring us to maturiity
God often has to allow suffering to enter our lives.

I experienced this acutely a few years ago when I
went in for a routine mammogram. I suspected something was wrong when the technician refused to meet
my gaze after she developed the films. Confirmation
of my suspicions came the next morning when my
doctor called.

"Hello, Nancy. This is Dr. Swann calling. How are
you this morning?"

"Well," I responded, "I can't be all right or you wouldn't be calling me. What did the mammogram show?"

"Unfortunately, it appears that you may have a problem–but we can't be sure until we do a biopsy. I'm calling to set up that appointment."

Thus began one of the most challenging experiences of my life. Because I was learning to depend on the Lord in all circumstances, this experience proved to be one of great blessing. Twenty-five years ago, if you had told me breast cancer could prove to be a blessing, I'd have thought you were crazy. However, the Lord used this experience to teach me a great deal about His *grace.*

Eventually a surgeon cut the carcinoma out of my body. *But God removed a much worse cancer.* He cut away forever that "cancer" named *fear.* Except for a very painful night immediately following the surgery, I felt nothing but peace throughout the experience of a *total mastectomy.*

The prayers and visits of family and Christian friends made me realize, as never before, the blessing of being in God's family. I had never realized just how many wonderful sisters and brothers in Christ God had given me until then.

I had never experienced directly the compassion of the professional staff of the hospital. Their gentle care helped me through that painful twenty-four hour period after surgery. They remained solicitous, despite my episodes of projectile vomiting. Never have I been more helpless. Never have I appreciated tender, gentle, competent hands so much.

Looking back, I can see how much I grew during that period. In a deeper way, I learned how *dependent* we are on one another. I learned what a gift good health and a properly functioning body are.

I learned how deeply I love my family and how much they love me. I learned how vain and foolish I had been about my "physical perfection" and fear that my husband's love was connected to my appearance.

Most importantly, I learned what God's grace can do for us as we struggle with some of life's most demanding challenges. God will be there for us, supplying grace in proportion to our needs–no matter how difficult life becomes, *if* we have established a solid relationship with Him as *Lord*, not Savior only!

We may ask, "Why doesn't God *always* answer our prayers?" But He does answer. Sometimes it is "No." Sometimes it is "Not yet." But He *always* whispers, "Trust me," in whatever He asks us to endure.

How we respond to such challenges determines whether we will shrink or grow through them. If we hold the Master's hand throughout our difficulties these words from the Psalms 103 (RSV) will be carved upon our heart:

Bless the Lord, O my soul: And all that is within me, bless His holy Name. Bless the Lord, O my soul, and forget not all His benefits: Who forgiveth all thine iniquities; who healeth all thy diseases; Who redeemeth thy life from destruction; who crowneth thee with lovingkindness and tender mercies; Who satisfieth thy mouth with good things; so that thy youth is renewed like the eagle's.

Does God always answer prayer? Yes! But sometimes His answer is, "No," or "Not yet." What can we do to increase the "Yes" answers?

Sometimes our sins are subtle and so deeply entrenched that we become oblivious to them.

The Word of God tells us to tithe–but how many of us actually do so?

Jesus said, *You cannot serve both God and money,* yet many of us try to do just that! When we withhold even a portion of our tithe, we erect a wall between ourselves and the power of God.

When we are not open to God's Spirit we become "duplicitous"–two-faced. Jesus is the only person who never practiced duplicity or two-facedness. That's why He could say, *I and the Father are One. I always do exactly what the Father tells me to do.*

While Jesus eschewed personal property; we *covet* and *collect* personal property. Jesus depended on His Father's providence to meet all His needs and had no place to lay His head. We depend on our *investment programs* and build bigger and better houses as a sign of our financial success.

"We spend money we do not have to buy things we do not need to impress people we do not like," says psychiatrist M. Scott Peck.

We may make a pledge to our church and/or favorite charity–but we always pay ourselves first. Few of us know much about "sacrificial giving," and few experience the full blessings such unselfish sharing brings.

We marvel at Mother Theresa when we see how unselfish and dedicated she is in helping the poor and downtrodden. Yet, this should be *normal* for a *true* disciple of Jesus Christ!

Whenever I see a news item about Mother Theresa, I cringe just a bit–recognizing how far I am from her total dedication.

Stewardship is the area in which most of us stumble. We can't quite "let go and let God."

Think what the Lord could do if everyone who professes to be a Christian not only tithed, but gave away all they did not *actually need* for their own day-to-day existence. We could eliminate poverty. We often wonder why God allows the suffering of the poverty-stricken. But I believe He is waiting for *us* to solve that problem.

Actually, the tithe is just the *minimum* we are to give to God. Whenever possible, we are to give *more* than the minimum ten percent.

Perhaps we are like the desperate man in the story who promised God that if He would find Him a job, he would gladly pay Him twenty-five percent of his wages. He got the job and for the first year faithfully gave a quarter of his earnings to the Lord.

Because he was a diligent worker he was soon promoted, then promoted again. With each new promotion came an increase in salary. Although he had originally been paid only $16,000 per year, by the end of three years he was making $40,000–but he didn't think he could afford to give the Lord $10,000 of it, so he began to "fudge" a bit on his promise. By the time he'd been with the company ten years, he was made a Vice President, and his salary was $100,000 a year–but he was only giving $8,000 of it to God's work in the world. Sadly, his promise of twenty-five percent long repressed and forgotten.

When we are "desperate," we make promises we fail to keep when we become prosperous. Then we wonder why we don't grow spiritually. We forget that we cannot serve two masters; either we will love the one and hate the other, or respect the one and despise the other. We cannot serve both God and money!

We are to give generosity, not begrudgingly.

One time I visited a family who had hired a mentally retarded teenager for the day to clean out their garage and basement. The young man worked diligently, clearing away trash, emptying ashes, bundling newspapers. Finally, close to 5:00 p.m., he came to the door and announced he had finished his job.

The man of the house told his wife to give the boy twenty-five cents, saying, "He won't know the difference, anyway!"

In spite of this gross injustice, the man expected God to answer his prayers promptly and generously. But God doesn't honor such mean-spirited hypocrisy. I suspect God has less trouble with an out-and-out atheist who is generous and fair to everyone than He does with penny-pinching Christians who would short-change someone if they think they can get away with it.

I have to confess, I'm guilty of hypocrisy, too. May God help me to become sensitive to the hypocrisy in my life and eliminate it completely! How about you? Is this a sin you need to confess and abandon?

Not only do some people fail to tithe their income, many fail miserably in tithing their *time*.

If we each gave ten percent of every twenty-four hours to God, we would spend almost two-and-a-half hours per day in worship and service–or about seventy-two hours, nearly *three full days* per month!

Many of us pray only at mealtimes and upon retiring, giving God just a token of devotion. As a matter of fact, much of the world has largely abandoned prayer–even simple prayer. And it does not even know that intercessory prayer is possible.

Until we learn to pray earnestly, and in intercession, our prayers are almost meaningless. Until one *experiences* God from the depths of his being, he does not truly "experience" Him at all.

When God exists only on our periphery, we must depend on "faith" to assure us He really exists at all. But when we have discovered Him in our own innermost being, we learn to know Him.

This degree of intimacy with God was well known at one time, but with the Reformation many well-meaning Protestants threw out the baby with the bath water when they set out to reform the Catholic Church. Along with penances, the purchase of indulgences, and confession, they also eliminated the practice of Christian meditation and contemplation. Until we arrive at an understanding and practice of these most meaningful ways to pray, few of our prayers will be the rich "at-one-ment," or communion experience prayer is really meant to be.

Among Protestants, the Quakers (Society of Friends) are remarkable for their continued practice of "*centering* prayer." This group is also remarkable for their compassionate outreach. I do not think this is a coincidence, for whenever we spend time in silence, waiting for God to speak, eventually this command comes through loud and clear: *Feed my sheep!*

Fearing today's New Age philosophies, many people are afraid of the practice of meditation and contemplation (waiting in silence for the Presence of God), fearing they lead to Quietism. In fact, just the opposite occurs.

Earnest prayer energizes us and fills us with joy and enthusiasm. It is the source of the "abundant life" Jesus means for us to experience. Christian meditation and contemplation require severe self-discipline, however, and are practiced by very few in our hurried, harried world.

Yet time spent in these disciplines orders all the rest of life. I have learned that one hour of prayer is worth two hours of sleep. This being true, we short-change ourselves when we elect to stay in bed rather than getting up an hour earlier to spend quiet time with the Lord.

Many will argue that they are not "morning persons" and prefer to pray in the afternoon or evening.

The poet Ralph Spaulding Cushman has responded to this attitude in his poem, *The Secret:*

I met God in the morning
When my day was at its best,
And His presence came like sunrise,
Like a glory in my breast.

All day long the Presence lingered,
All day long He stayed with me,
And we sailed in perfect calmness
O'er a very troubled sea.

Other ships were blown and battered,
Other ships were sore distressed,
But the winds that seemed to drive them
Brought to us a peace and rest.

Then I thought of other mornings,
With a keen remorse of mind,
When I, too, had loosed the moorings,
With the Presence left behind.

So I think I know the secret,
Learned from many a troubled way:
You must seek Him in the morning
If you want Him through the day!

Jesus tells us: *Seek ye first the Kingdom of God and His righteousness, and all these things shall be added unto you.* (Matt. 6:33)

He also tells us, *The Kingdom of Heaven is within you.* (Luke 17:21)

To discover the Kingdom Within, we must experience communion with God's Spirit.

When I first began to "investigate prayer," I knew of no one else who truly communed with God's Spirit in prayer. Since then I have met many other Christians who know the secret of "practicing the presence." They all concur that this is life's single most satisfying experience. Many, many hymns have been written about it ("Sweet Hour of Prayer," "What a Friend We Have in Jesus," "In the Garden," etc.).

There is no greater experience than sitting with God and drinking in His sublime Presence. And it is equally available to all–it requires no special intellect, equipment, or education. All it needs is the love of God and your time!

Some Christians see such extended prayer as a waste of time. But there is no *better* investment of time and energy. As one song puts it: "Give God His due, and God will give back to you, and turn your water into wine."

We can *never* out give God! Everything we give to Him comes back to us several times over. No matter what we give to Him (love, time, money, praise) it will be given back to us "pressed down and running over." It is a wonderful form of "frustration" to try to give to God without getting more in return. It cannot be done.

This is as true of our time as of everything else. Give God the first two hours of your day and you will be amazed at how He multiplies the productivity of the remaining hours of labor.

In order to become a *prayer warrior,* one has to believe that God exists and that He rewards those who diligently search for Him. (See Hebrews 11:6.)

In Proverbs we read, *The fear of the Lord is the beginning of wisdom.* But in I John 4:18 we are told, ***Perfect love casteth out fear.***

And James 1:5-8 tells us, *If anyone lacks wisdom, he should ask God, who gives generously to all without finding fault, and it will be given to him. But when he asks, he must believe and not doubt, because he who doubts is like a wave of the sea, blown and tossed by the wind. That man should not think he will receive anything from the Lord; he is a double-minded man, unstable in all he does.* (NIV)

If you have not received *abundant* answers to your prayers, perhaps your faith is too weak. To strengthen our faith we need to:

1. *Pray* for greater faith. ("Lord, I believe. Help Thou my unbelief.")

2. Recommit yourself to the Lord. (If you're not sure you *are* a Christian, see the Prayer of Salvation in the next chapter and pray accordingly.)

3. Begin to tithe not just your money, but your time and talents as well. (Spend one hour upon arising in prayer and devotion, half an hour at noon, and one hour in the evening.) Ask God to show you *His* plan for your life–He wants to use your gifts in building His Kingdom.

4. Regularly *thank God* for His gifts, His care, and His guidance. Spend at least 30 minutes every day in praise and gratitude.

5. Pray for miracles *and expect them!*

Again, let me remind you, there is nothing special about *me.* I am just an ordinary sinner like everyone else. But there is something very special about Jesus Christ! It is He who sends the Holy Spirit to us and

He who intercedes on our behalf with the Father.

. . . If God be for us, who can be against us?
(Romans 8:31)

Because of what *He* has done, we may come to the Father in His name and *expect results*. It is through Him our prayers are answered. Prayer is the vital connection to God's transforming power because of what Jesus has accomplished, not because of what you or I have done or will do.

If each night we empty out our "cup of sin" at the foot of the cross, asking God's forgiveness for it, *he is faithful and just to forgive us our sins, and to cleanse us from all unrighteousness.* (I John 1:9)

Then if we go to Him first thing in the morning, kneeling at the foot of the cross, and present our "empty cup," He will fill it with *one day's worth of grace*-never more, but never less. This we must do every day for the rest of our lives! God's grace is sufficient *when we avail ourselves of the means of grace*. Remember when the Hebrews gathered manna in the wilderness? If they gathered more than one day's supply, it rotted over night. I believe God gives one day's supply of grace at a time.

Jesus Himself fasted-once for 40 days and nights-and He told the disciples when their efforts were ineffective, *This kind (of demon) comes not out except by **prayer and fasting.***

If we want consistent answers to prayer we, too, need to fast when appropriate. Not only does fasting show our seriousness and sincerity, it also frees up at least an hour a day–even more if you are the cook–which can then be spent in additional prayer. (Those who are diabetic or have low blood sugar should not fast unless their physician approves, but they can limit their eating accordingly. You need to be in good physical condition before undertaking any serious fast.)

I try to fast at least one day a week–but often fail, and even when I succeed I seem to make up for it the next day. But fasting *is* a sign of our seriousness with God. We ought to be willing and able to give up at least one day's meals a week. (If everyone observed a one day fast each week, and contributed the money they would have spent on food to world hunger, we could help eliminate it.)

Let me repeat: all prayer is answered if we are truly in Christ, but some prayers are answered, "No," or "Not yet."

When my oldest son married, I began to anticipate grandchildren. When four years had passed with no sign of a child, I began to pray for one. But God ignored my prayers.

After seven years, that marriage failed–and I thanked God He had refused my request. That experience was extremely painful for my son (and us), but it would have been much harder had there been children involved. God's timing is perfect and He is still Sovereign. We must be willing to let God be God and not try to run the world for Him!

We need to *thank* God for, "No," and "Not yet," answers, too!

For Reflection

Unanswered Prayer

"An all-pervading goodness and love can only take on meaning when that perfection is broken and there is an encounter with their opposites: anti-goodness and anti-love. Logical necessity, therefore, requires a measure of suffering and evil in the world in order that the positive qualities of love and goodness should be allowed to assume meaning."

Russell Stannard
Science and the Renewal of Belief

"It is not God who creates the evil; He merely opens up the possibility of our rejecting Him; it is then our act of rejection that creates the evil; evil is our responsibility."

Ibid.

"Could the experience of pain and disease make the fact of death concrete for us, and therefore an awakening force?"

Jacob Needleman
A Sense of the Cosmos

Questions for Discussion

Chapter Eleven

1. Can you cite, in retrospect, any prayers answered, "No," or "Not yet," where the answer proved a blessing in disguise?

2. How do we explain to our children when their prayers are answered, "No," or "Not yet,"?

3. Should we pray less so we'll have fewer disappointments?

4. Do you think God may answer the requests of those who make prayer their *first resource* more often or more promptly than those who make it their *last resort?* Why or why not?

References

Unanswered Prayer

Genesis 13:8-9
Psalms 37:7-16
Psalms 41:1-3
Proverbs 19:17; 21:13, 25-27; 22:1-4, 8
Ecclesiastes 5:8-17
Isaiah 58:4-9
Matthew 6:5-34
Matthew 9:10-13
Matthew 19:16-30
Mark 9:29
Mark 12:38-44
Luke 2:37
Luke 6:27-38
Luke 12:33-3 4
Luke 18:10-14
Luke 20:45-47
II Corinthians 9:6-15
Ephesians 5:3-9
Philippians 4:4-7, 11-19
I Timothy 6:9-10
James 2:1-10
I Peter 3:7
I John 3:13-18, 21-24
Jude 1:10-11

Notes

Chapter Twelve

Prayer:
The Great Equalizer

Faith and Obedience:
Keys to Answered Prayer

He that hath my commandments, and keepeth them, he it is that loveth me: and he that loveth me shall be loved of my Father, and I will love him, and will manifest myself to him.

John 14:21

. . . If a man loves me, he will keep my words (commandments): and my Father will love him, and we will come unto him, and make our abode with him. He that loveth me not keepeth not my sayings: . . .

John 14:23, 24A

183

If ye abide in me, and my words abide in you, ye shall ask what you will, and it shall be done unto you.

John 15:7

Americans are taught that all men are created equal–but that's not true. Some of us are brighter or stronger or more beautiful or more talented than our brothers and sisters, and some of us are less so. Yet, it is true that we should all have equal opportunity under the law *to make the most of what we do have.*

When we function under *God's* plan, we have equal opportunity through *prayer,* "The Great Equalizer." Each of us has equal opportunity to avail ourselves of God's power, His intervention, and His plan for our lives. (*With God all things are possible,* says Matthew19:26.)

Through His power, God can make up for any deficit we feel in our intellect, our appearance, our strength, or our talents. His grace is equally available to all.

Trust and obey
For there's no other way
To be happy in Jesus
But to TRUST and OBEY!

Remember, in John 15 Jesus says, *I am the vine and you are the branches. If a man remains in me and I in him, he will bear much fruit; apart from me you can do nothing. If anyone does not remain in me, he is like a branch that is thrown away and withers;*

such branches are picked up, thrown into the fire, and burned. If you remain in me and my words remain in you, ask whatever you wish, and it will be given you. (Paraphrased)

If we spend time each day in the Word and *commit key passages to memory* we then have Christ's words abiding in us. Frequent repetition of, and meditation upon, the words of Jesus act to fan the flames of love and obedience to the Holy Spirit within us.

Many of us have ceased daily Scripture reading and regular times for conversation with God. Few of our children are required to memorize Scripture, and few adults remember what they once knew–because they have failed to reinforce it. Yet, Jesus Himself emphasized the importance of His "Words of Life."

Words are like seeds. Planted in the soil of our minds, they bear fruit. Plant trashy words, cultivate trashy words; reap trashy thoughts, trashy acts. Plant noble words, cultivate noble words; reap noble thoughts, noble acts.

When neither the home nor the school takes responsibility for instilling the Words of Life, life becomes impoverished. Our children become impoverished. Our society becomes impoverished if its individual members cease abiding in Jesus and no longer cultivate His words within themselves.

There is, as far as I know, only one sure way to teach children to pray: pray with them! When do you start? Right away!

Even in utero, infants can hear spoken words *and* feel changes in the mother's vital signs which occur during extended times of prayer (lowered heart rate, slower breathing, a general calming and quieting of the body.)

When children grow up hearing mother and father praying regularly, they will pray regularly and naturally. In addition to grace at mealtimes and bedtime prayers said as a family, each parent also needs serious, private time *alone with God.* When small children are taught to respect mother's and father's private quiet time, they realize very early that prayer is an important priority in the Christian life.

One cannot *tell* the child to pray and expect them to do so unless and until you have established a deep, regular prayer life of your own.

Children do what we do, not what we say we do. If we talk about the importance of prayer, but do not pray, that's exactly what our children will do. They will learn by our example to "*talk* a good show" rather than *show* a good talk with the Lord.

Prayer time with small children is extremely important. A quiet time of prayer with each child at bedtime (without siblings present) is one way to establish a stronger bond between you and the child; it also establishes their bond with Jesus Christ and strengthens it daily as the child grows (physically, mentally, emotionally, *and* spiritually.)

Prayer: The Great Equalizer

One of my deepest regrets in raising my own children is that I failed to teach them when they were *tiny and moldable* the art and practice of prayer. But because I became a Christian late in life, I didn't know how to pray *myself*–until they were all in school. I do hope *and pray* that their observation of *my* attention to prayer will leave a lasting impression upon them.

Children sense that prayer is either our *first resource* or our *last resort,* and are deeply influenced even when we say little or nothing to them about the importance of prayer. Prayer and Bible study have always been the signs of a serious walk with Jesus Christ.

Let me stress again that our children will do as we do, not as we say! If we merely *say* prayer and Bible study and its application are important, but do not practice what we preach, they will grow up just *talking* about prayer and Bible study, and not doing it.

On the other hand, if they are witness to our prayers and our hunger and thirst for spiritual food, they will develop accordingly. Over the years, my children have seen numerous answers to prayer, some of them highly significant, and even amazing, some of them relatively trivial. What matters is that they have heard me pray about almost everything at one time or another. Then they have witnessed God's answers. These observations do more to teach them the importance of our prayers and *God's faithfulness* than all the preaching in the world could do.

What kinds of answers have they seen?

One time my husband had misplaced the licenses for our sailboat. He started looking for them about 9:00 a.m. on the first day of the sailing season, but by nearly 11:00 a.m. he had not found them.

The licenses had come in the mail back in February. He remembered having received them, but had no idea where he had put them. In order to be out on the lake in time for the race he needed to leave the house by 12:00.

At 10:50, Brian came into the kitchen where I was working and said, "Mom, why don't you pray that Dad will find that license so we can go sailing this afternoon?"

He and I together bowed our heads and asked the Lord to show us where the licenses were. We had no sooner lifted our heads when the thought popped into my mind, "Look in his books." So I sent Brian to ask his father what books he had been reading since the licenses had arrived.

A few minutes later, Brian reappeared telling me that all his father's books and journals from the first of the year were stacked on the floor in his closet. Brian was going to go look through them. I went back to my work in the kitchen and promptly forgot all about the missing boat license. But at 11:55, Brian came "flying" into the kitchen waving the licenses over his head.

"Hey Mom, why didn't God tell you they were in the last one?" he exclaimed.

Why indeed? What had gone on in this process? Was it God who answered my prayer, or only my own unconscious which could have rightly deduced that my husband might have stuck them in a book, since that's the kind of thing I might have done myself? All I can say is, I don't know, but I considered it God's doing, and *so did our children!*

In Matthew 7 we are reminded, *Not all who sound religious are really Godly people. They may refer to me as Lord, but still won't get to heaven, for the important thing is whether they obey my Father in heaven. At the judgment many will tell me, 'Lord, we told others about you and used your name to cast out demons and do many other miracles!' but I will reply, 'You have never been mine. Depart from me. I NEVER KNEW YOU.* (LB)

Maybe we don't often get ready answers to our prayers because we no longer "abide daily," no longer let His words "abide in us," no longer are diligent in prayer, Bible study, and acts of obedience or charity. Or maybe we don't *really* know Him.

Perhaps we need to return to the Godliness and "fear of the Lord" our fathers and grandfathers practiced. What do you think? Are you zealous in your devotion to Jesus? Or are you "lukewarm?" I wonder what would happen if we all made prayer and Bible study one of our highest priorities again?

Remember, growth in prayer begins with these three prayers:

1. Prayer for an ever-deepening relationship with Jesus Christ, asking God to help you surrender your *entire will* to Him.

2. Prayer for a fresh infilling by the Holy Spirit and for wisdom and insight as you study the Scriptures showing you how you should respond to them.

3. Prayer for *discipline and self-control* as God reveals His will for your life and as you struggle (and it will be a struggle sometimes!) to make what you do measure up to what you know.

We establish a close relationship with God exactly as we establish one with anyone else–*by spending time with Him.* The more quality time we spend with the Lord, the closer we will feel to Him. When we love someone, it is a delight to be in their presence–we want to be with them.

Exciting answers to prayer motivate us to spend more and more time with our Lord and Savior. All those we love will be blessed by our communion!

Many times we feel too rushed and too busy to spend more than five minutes a day with God. Such superficial devotion rarely brings about a close walk with the Lord. Often we put God back on the shelf when we return the Bible to the shelf. We need to take

Him with us wherever we go! He's *always* there, of course, but often ignored.

We cannot get away from God–even though we think we have. We may be oblivious to God's presence, but He is never really absent from us, whether we acknowledge His presence or not.

We can't make God a mere incidental in our crowded schedule and still expect Him to honor our requests. He wants to permeate us and our world completely. Until we allow Him to go everywhere with us, we won't experience the full peace and pleasure of His presence, and our prayers may seem to go unanswered.

Make God an integral part of all you do and watch your world change. Such devotion leads to the full abundant life of joy Jesus died to bring us. A life of stunted devotion becomes a stunted life.

No one wants a stunted life.

We must learn to love God *even more than we love our spouse, our children or grandchildren, our fiancee, our career, that boyfriend or girlfriend, or anyone or anything else*. That may seem hard to do. How do we get to love God that way? *The same way we learn to love anyone else: we spend time with Him, quality time*. You can't love anyone until you get to know them, and you can't get to know them if you won't spend time with them.

If you are not sure you *are* a Christian you *can* be sure! You need to acknowledge that you are a sinner–we *all* are! And there is no way to bridge the gap between God and humankind, except by Grace through the sacramental death of Jesus Christ on the cross.

You need to:
1. Confess your sin to God.
2. Accept Jesus Christ as your Savior, and
3. Receive the free gift of Salvation by Grace.

Pray the three prayers listed above and remember, all prayer must be consistent with the Will of God.

There is *no other way to salvation.* My early personal study of religion helped me realize how much I needed a Savior. Most religions recognize that man is "off course" or "out of step" with God. Most provide elaborate and complex methods for "enlightenment" which require several lifetimes to achieve. *But enlightenment is not salvation!*

I would never have achieved salvation if left to achieve it on my own merits. I know how imperfect I am–despite my efforts at self-improvement.

Below is my *prayer of salvation:*

"Dear Lord Jesus, I confess I am a sinner by nature. But I want to go your way. Thank you for giving your life for me. Thank you for forgiving my sins. Please take control of my life, and help me to live as I should. Thank you for your wonderful gift of eternal life. Thank you for making it possible for me to become a child of God, in spite of my past mistakes and my flawed character."

Do you need to pray this prayer?

Jesus really is *the way, the truth, and the life.* (John 14:6) No one comes to the Father, but by Him. Only Jesus Christ is able to finally and fully forgive men their sins.

Once we know our salvation is secure, we then need to work *out* what God has worked *in*. (See Philippians 2:12.)

Many people in mainline Protestant churches know little about the Bible–and they don't seem to care to know any more. They have somehow lost sight of the treasures contained in the Scriptures. Perhaps their self-sufficiency has made God's Word of little value to them.

Since many of them are highly educated professional people, they perhaps don't feel they need God. Many of them seem to believe in Religion rather than in God. And some of them believe *in* God without *believing God.*

This brings us to the all-important subject of Grace. No matter how diligent we are, we cannot *force* God to respond to us. In the final analysis, *Grace is everything.*

"I will be kind to whom I choose," God has said.

I know many people who are more "worthy" (*none* of us is really worthy) of God's blessings than I am; I am at a loss to explain why He has so richly answered my prayers. Certainly He knew long before I did that I would one day write this book; perhaps my prayers were answered so that I might encourage others to pray. Or perhaps I have had more prayers answered because I *have prayed more prayers*.

The person who prays one prayer a day has only one chance for answered prayer. The person who prays about *everything* is bound, just by the law of averages, to have more prayers answered "yes." Increase your prayers, and you will doubtless increase the number of answers you receive.

To test this out, get a small spiral notebook in which to record your prayer requests. Then, just as Carrie did, record in red the date that prayer is answered. At the end of the year you will be amazed to see what the Lord has done in your life.

At the end of your life He will have made your life a work of art. Life *is* what you make it, but with Jesus Christ it not only will become beautiful–it will endure forever. He makes all things beautiful in His time, and a thing of beauty *is* a joy forever!

Referred to as the *Our Father* by many or *The Lord's Prayer* by many others, this prayer taught to the disciples by our Lord should probably be called the "Disciples' Prayer." (Matthew 6:9-13)

Although millions of Christians have learned it and committed it to memory, Jesus *probably* meant for it to be used as a model prayer rather than one to be recited verbatim. He did warn us *not* to recite the same words over and over again, as the Pharisees did, but to speak to God from our hearts.

How can we make this great prayer our model? Let's look at it to see.

Our Father which art in heaven, Hallowed be thy name. To hallow (make or recognize as holy) is to give appropriate respect and recognition to God. If we use this statement as a model, we will begin our prayer with words of awe, love, and reverence for God: "Oh God, you who are perfect in wisdom, love, and knowledge, you whose name is above every name, you who are perfect in righteousness, justice, *and* mercy, you who made the earth, the sun, the moon, the stars, and everything that is, our Father, Savior, Master, and Lord . . ." might be a beginning statement.

Then we would go on to the next phrase:

Thy kingdom come. Thy will be done in earth, as it is in Heaven, which we might express in a manner similar to this: "Help us in general, and me in particular, to make decisions and choices which will cause your Kingdom to be realized more nearly in my own life, and the lives of those I influence. Help me to make this a heaven on earth for my loved ones, friends, colleagues, and associates. Help me to so treat people that they will know I have spent time with you, my Lord and Savior . . . ."

Then *Give us this day our daily bread* may become: "Thank you for all the wonderful foods you have provided for us; please grant that we'll have enough for our needs, but not *more* than we need, and help us to make decisions and choices which will make it possible for everyone in the world to have enough. Give us wisdom as we distribute and use all the resources you have so graciously provided. Help us to see that none of your children go hungry anywhere in the world."

And forgive us our debts (sins), as we forgive our debtors could be translated into: "Forgive me for my outburst of temper last night, and for my failure to respond positively to my daughter's request for help on her school paper, for being so cross to my spouse, and for any other ways I've been inconsiderate or mean to them. Forgive me for spending more time watching TV than I spent with you or my children today. Help me to change and humbly ask their forgiveness as I now ask yours."

And lead us not into temptation, but deliver us from evil; might become: "Father, help me to resist the temptation to overeat and help me to avoid too much TV or other time-wasting evils."

For thine is the kingdom, and the power, and the glory, forever could be expressed: "You are my Lord and Savior, my King. Help me to advance your kingdom in my home and community. Use your power to help us bring justice here and now, and may all we do and say glorify your Holy Name now and for eternity."

Each day our prayer will follow Jesus' "model prayer," but each day we will speak of the specific sins and blessings which we are experiencing. No two days will be exactly the same, of course, which will eliminate "rote recitation." We will naturally avoid this pitfall.

I don't believe it is *wrong* to recite the Lord's (or Disciples') Prayer, but it *can* become mere routine and less meaningful than specific prayer based on the Lord's Prayer as our pattern.

Prayer should be personal and specific. It should effect *change*-either in us or in those for whom we pray, or both. Ultimately, prayer should change us day by day into the image of Jesus Christ.

Not many of us will complete this process this side of the grave. But some will.

An American tourist in India stood by in awe as he watched Mother Theresa lovingly clean the infected wounds of a horribly disfigured leper.

"Sister," he commented, "I wouldn't do that for a million dollars!"

Her response?

"Neither would I, brother. Neither would I."

Remember, prayer is the vital connection to God's transforming power. It is through **Scriptural Prayer** that we can attain **Spiritual Power** in our life**!**

For Reflection

Prayer: The Great Equalizer

"Unless you are prepared to conduct your own individual search for God, you will not find Him. Religious understanding comes not from any argument based on another's experience, but from your own personal involvement."

Russell Stannard
Science and the Renewal of Belief, Pg. 101

"Just as you cannot be argued into loving another person, so you cannot expect to be argued into a loving relationship with God."

Ibid., Pg. 103

"The religious genius experiences the divine presence in the stillness of his own heart, in the deepest recesses of his soul. But it is always the reverential and trustful consciousness of the living presence of God, which is the keynote of the genuine prayer experience. It is true that the God to whom the worshipper cries transcends all material things–and yet the pious man feels His nearness with an assurance as undoubted as though a living man stood next to him."

Friedrich Heiler
The Essence of Prayer, Pg. 311

"We either see the evidence for God everywhere, or nowhere."

Paul Davies
God and the New Physics

I can never be lost to your spirit! I can never get away from God.

Psalms 139:7-8

For the foolishness of God is wiser than man's wisdom, and the weakness of God is stronger than man's strength.

I Corinthians 1:25

Then they asked Him, "What must we do to do the work God requires?" Jesus answered, "The work of God is this: to believe in the one He has sent."

John 6:28-29

Questions for Discussion

Chapter Twelve

1. If Scriptural Prayer is the key to Scriptural Power; then why do we neglect it?

2. What "equalization" through God's intervention does your personality, character, or physical body require?

3. Read the ninth chapter of John. Is there anything in the life of your family that God might be longing to "turn to His glory?" Is He waiting for your permission and/or your request to work a miracle?

4. If you were Joni Earickson Tada, would you have become a radiant witness to the power of God's grace in her circumstances? Why or why not?

5. Has *your* prayer life been energized by reading this book? Are you learning to "abide daily?" Remember to go to the foot of the cross every night and pour out your "cup of sin;" then return every morning to the foot of the cross and request that God fill your cup with one

day's worth of grace. Do this consistently
and watch God work in *your* life and the lives
of those you love!

$$\boxed{\textbf{Notes}}$$

Books by Starburst Publishers
(Partial listing—full list available on request)

A Woman's Guide To Spiritual Power   —Nancy L. Dorner

Subtitled: Through Scriptural Prayer. Do your prayers seem to go "against a brick wall"? Does God sometimes seem far away or non-existent? If your answer is "Yes, You are not alone. Prayer must be the cornerstone of your relationship to God. "This book is a powerful tool for anyone who is serious about prayer and discipleship"—Florence Littauer

(trade paper) ISBN 0914984470   **$9.95**

Dragon Slaying For Parents   —Tom Prinz, M.S.

Subtitled: Removing The Excess Baggage So You Can Be The Parent You Want To Be. Shows how Dragons such as Codependency, Low Self-Esteem and other hidden factors interfere with effective parenting. This book by a marriage, family, and child conselor, is for all parents—to assist them with the difficult task of raising responsible and confident children in the 1990's. It is written especially for parents who believe they have "tried everything!"

(trade paper) ISBN 0914984357   **$9.95**

Except For A Staff   —Randy R. Spencer

Parallels the various functions of the Old Testament shepherd's staff with the ever-present ministry of the Holy Spirit. It sheds new light on the role of the Holy Spirit in the life of the Christian. "You will be blessed and challenged through reading Except For A Staff," Rev. Jerry Falwell.

(trade paper) ISBN 0914984349   **$7.95**

The Quest For Truth   —Ken Johnson

A book designed to lead the reader to a realization that there is no solution to the world's problems, nor is there a purpose to life, apart from Jesus Christ. It is the story of a young man on a symbolic journey in search of happiness and the meaning of life.

(trade paper) ISBN 0914984217   **$7.95**

The Beast Of The East   —Alvin M. Shifflett

Asks the questions: Has the Church become involved in a 'late date' comfort mode—expecting to be 'raptured' before the Scuds fall? Should we prepare for a lonmg and arduous Desert Storm to Armageddon battle? Are we ignoring John 16:33, *"In this world you will have trouble?"* (NIV)

(trade paper) ISBN 0914984411   **$6.95**

Like A Bulging Wall   —Robert Borrud

Will you survive the 1990's economic crash? This book shows how debt, greed, and covetousness, along with a lifestyle beyond our means, has brought about an explosive situation in this country. Gives "call" from God to prepare for judgement in America, Also lists TOP-RATED U.S. BANKS and SAVINGS & LOANS.

(trade paper) ISBN 0914984284   **$8.95**

Books by Starburst Publishers—cont'd.

Courting The King Of Terrors
—Frank Carl
with Joan Hake Roble

Why are so many people turning to Mental, Spiritual and Physical suicide? This book probes the relentless ills that are destroying the American family, and offers counsel to families in crisis. "I know about suicide," says Frank Carl. "I lost a Brother and a Sister to that monster!"

(trade paper) ISBN 0914984187 **$7.95**

Man And Wife For Life
—Joseph Kanzlemar, Ed.D.

A penetrating and often humorous look into real life situations of married people. Helps the reader get a new understanding of the problems and relationships within marriage.

(trade paper) ISBN 0914984233 **$7.95**

A Candle In Darkness (novel)
—June Livesay

A heartwarming novel (based on fact), set in the mountains of Ecuador. This book is filled with love, suspense, and intrigue. The first in a series of books by June Livesay.

(trade paper) ISBN 0914984225 **$8.95**

Devotion in Motion
—Joan Hake Robie

Worship in a new dimension! Leads the reader into a deeper, more creative experience of worship.

(trade paper) ISBN 0914984004 **$4.95**

You Can Live In Divine Health
—Joyce Boisseau

Medical and Spiritual considerations concerning the dilemma of sickness. "Does the Christian have an inherited right to divine health?"

(trade paper) ISBN 0914984020 **$6.95**

Purchasing Information

Listed books are available from your favorite Bookstore, either from current stock or special order. You may also order direct from STARBURST PUBLISHERS. When ordering enclose full payment plus $2.00* for shipping and handling ($2.50* if Canada or Overseas). Payment in US Funds only. Please allow two to three weeks minimum (longer overseas) for delivery. Make checks payable to and mail to STARBURST PUBLISHERS, P.O. Box 4123, LANCASTER, PA 17604. **Prices subject to change without notice**. Catalog available upon request.

* We reserve the right to ship your order the least expensive way. If you desire first class (domestic) or air shipment (overseas) please enclose shipping funds as follows: First Class within the USA enclose $4.00, Airmail Canada enclose $5.00, and Overseas enclose 30% (minimum $5.00) of total order. All remittance must be in US Funds.   07-92